GRAPHIC LIBRARY™

GRAPHIC SCIENCE

THE *EXPLOSIVE* WORLD OF VOLCANOES

WITH MAX AXIOM™ SUPER SCIENTIST

An Augmented Reading Science Experience

by Christopher L. Harbo | illustrated by Tod Smith

Consultant:
Professor Kenneth
Department of Geology
School of Ocean and Earth Science
University of Hawaii, Honolulu

CAPSTONE PRESS
a capstone imprint

Graphic Library is published by Capstone Press,
1710 Roe Crest Drive, North Mankato, Minnesota 56003.
www.mycapstone.com

Library of Congress Cataloging-in-Publication Data is available on the Library of
Congress website.

ISBN: 978-1-5435-2947-0 (library binding)
ISBN: 978-1-5435-2958-6 (paperback)
ISBN: 978-1-5435-2968-5 (eBook PDF)

Summary: In graphic novel format, follows the adventures of Max Axiom as
he explains the science behind volcanoes.

Art Director and Designer
Bob Lentz

Colorist
Matt Webb

Cover Artist
Tod Smith

Editor
Christopher L. Harbo

Photo Credits
Capstone Studio/Karon Dubke: 29

Download the Capstone app!

- Ask an adult to download the Capstone 4D app.

- Scan the cover and stars inside the book for additional content.

When you scan a spread, you'll find fun extra stuff
to go with this book! You can also find these things
on the web at www.capstone4D.com using the
password: volcano.28470

TABLE OF CONTENTS

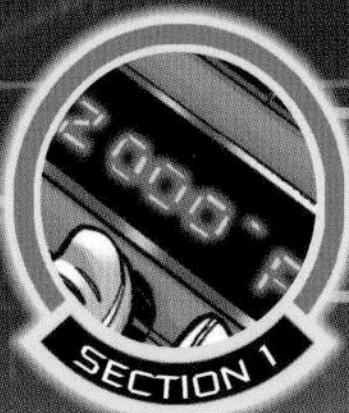
SECTION 1

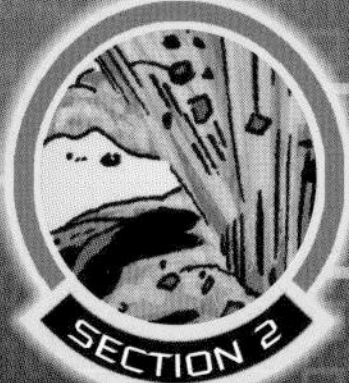
SECTION 2

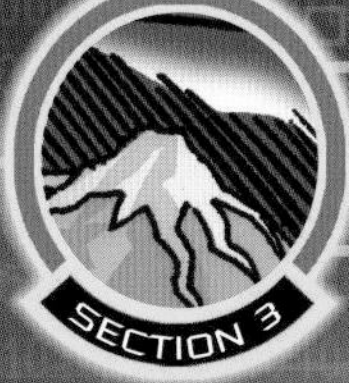
SECTION 3

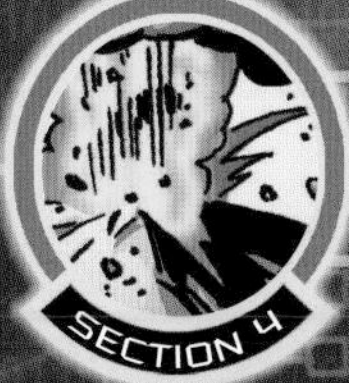
SECTION 4

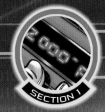

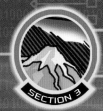

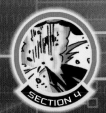

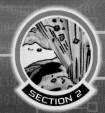

SECTION 1 EARTH'S INFERNO

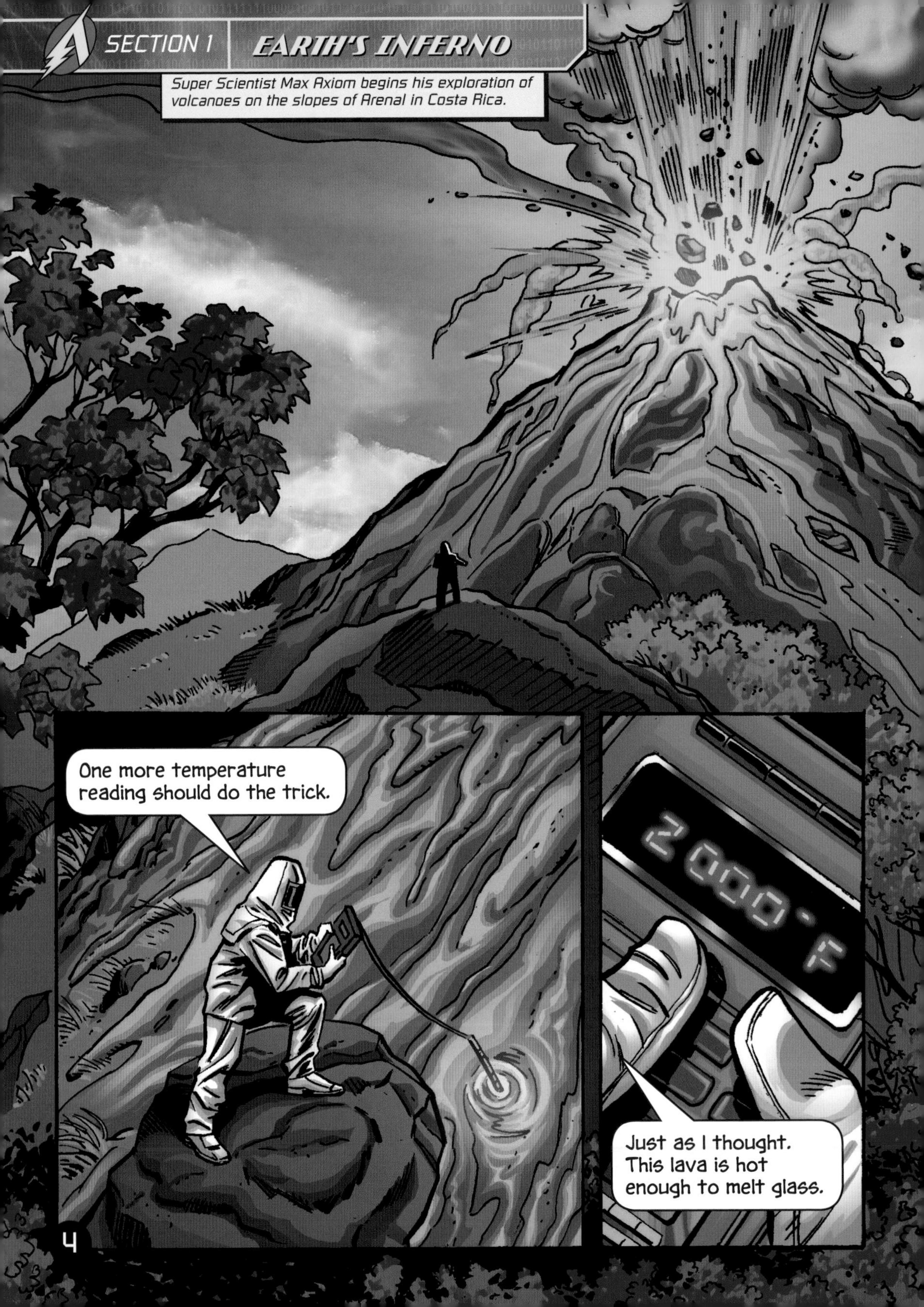

Super Scientist Max Axiom begins his exploration of volcanoes on the slopes of Arenal in Costa Rica.
One more temperature reading should do the trick.
2000°F
Just as I thought. This lava is hot enough to melt glass.

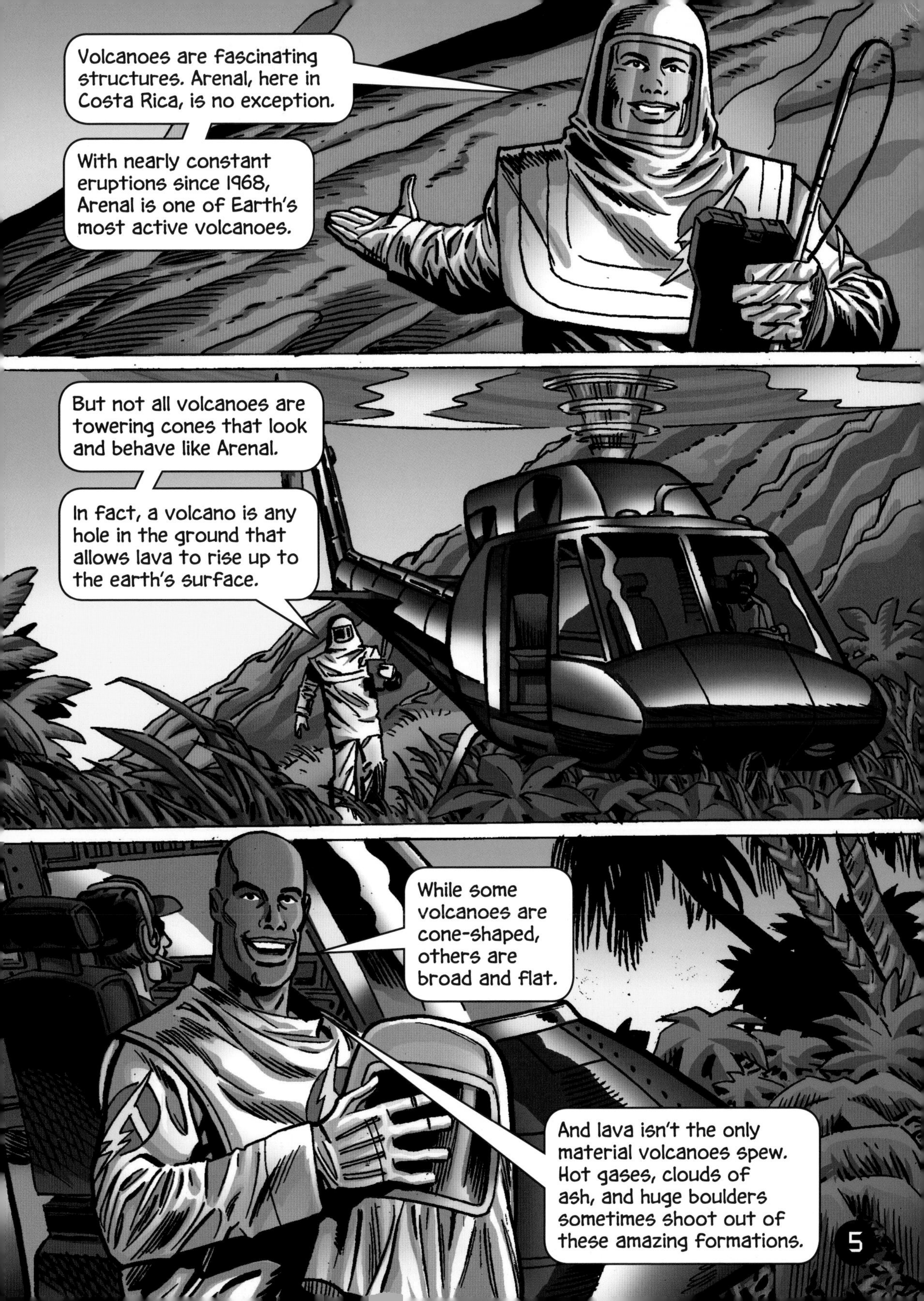
Volcanoes are fascinating structures. Arenal, here in Costa Rica, is no exception.
With nearly constant eruptions since 1968, Arenal is one of Earth's most active volcanoes.
But not all volcanoes are towering cones that look and behave like Arenal.
In fact, a volcano is any hole in the ground that allows lava to rise up to the earth's surface.
While some volcanoes are cone-shaped, others are broad and flat.
And lava isn't the only material volcanoes spew. Hot gases, clouds of ash, and huge boulders sometimes shoot out of these amazing formations.

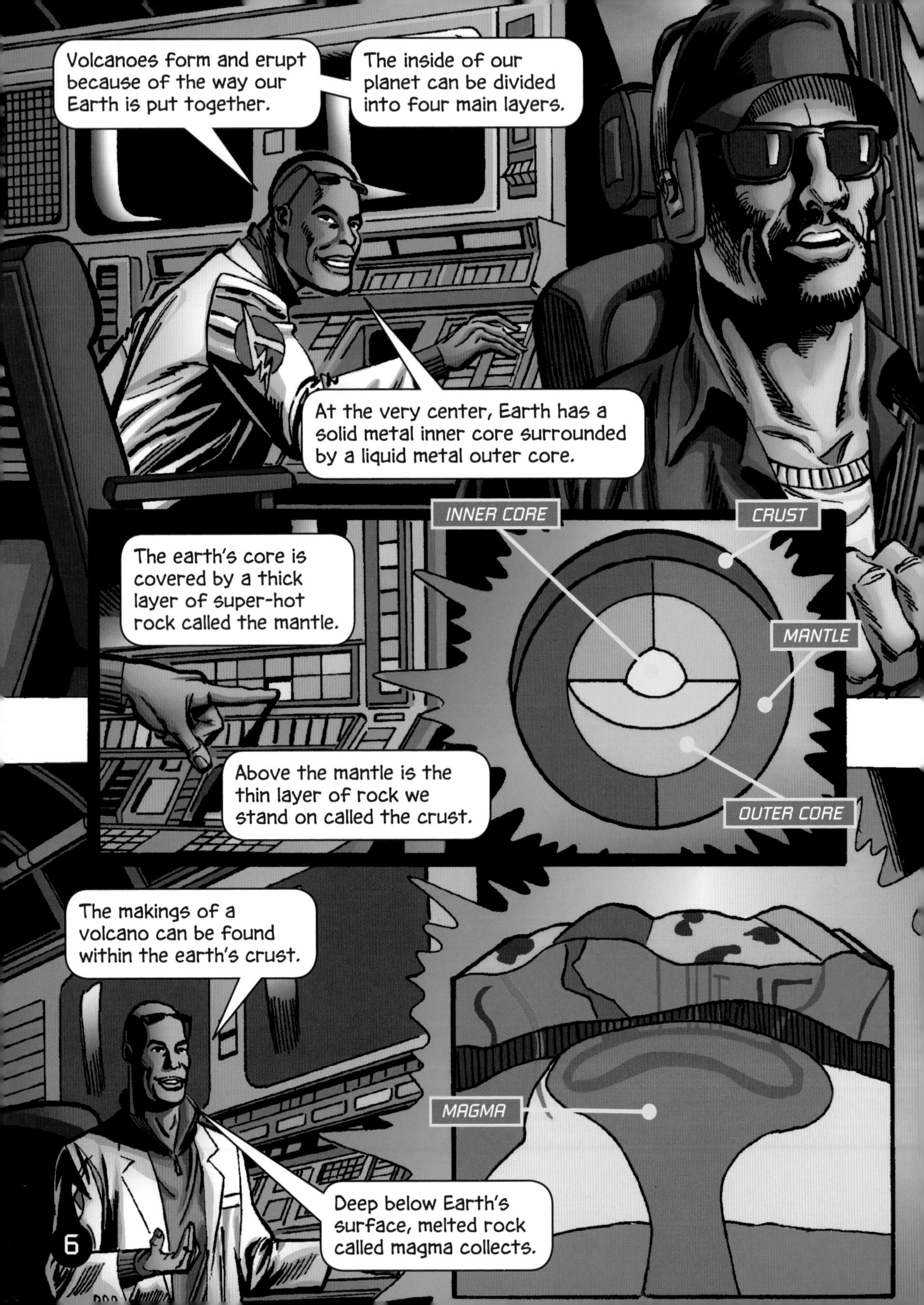
Volcanoes form and erupt because of the way our Earth is put together.
The inside of our planet can be divided into four main layers.
At the very center, Earth has a solid metal inner core surrounded by a liquid metal outer core.
The earth's core is covered by a thick layer of super-hot rock called the mantle.
INNER CORE
CRUST
MANTLE
OUTER CORE
Above the mantle is the thin layer of rock we stand on called the crust.
The makings of a volcano can be found within the earth's crust.
MAGMA
Deep below Earth's surface, melted rock called magma collects.

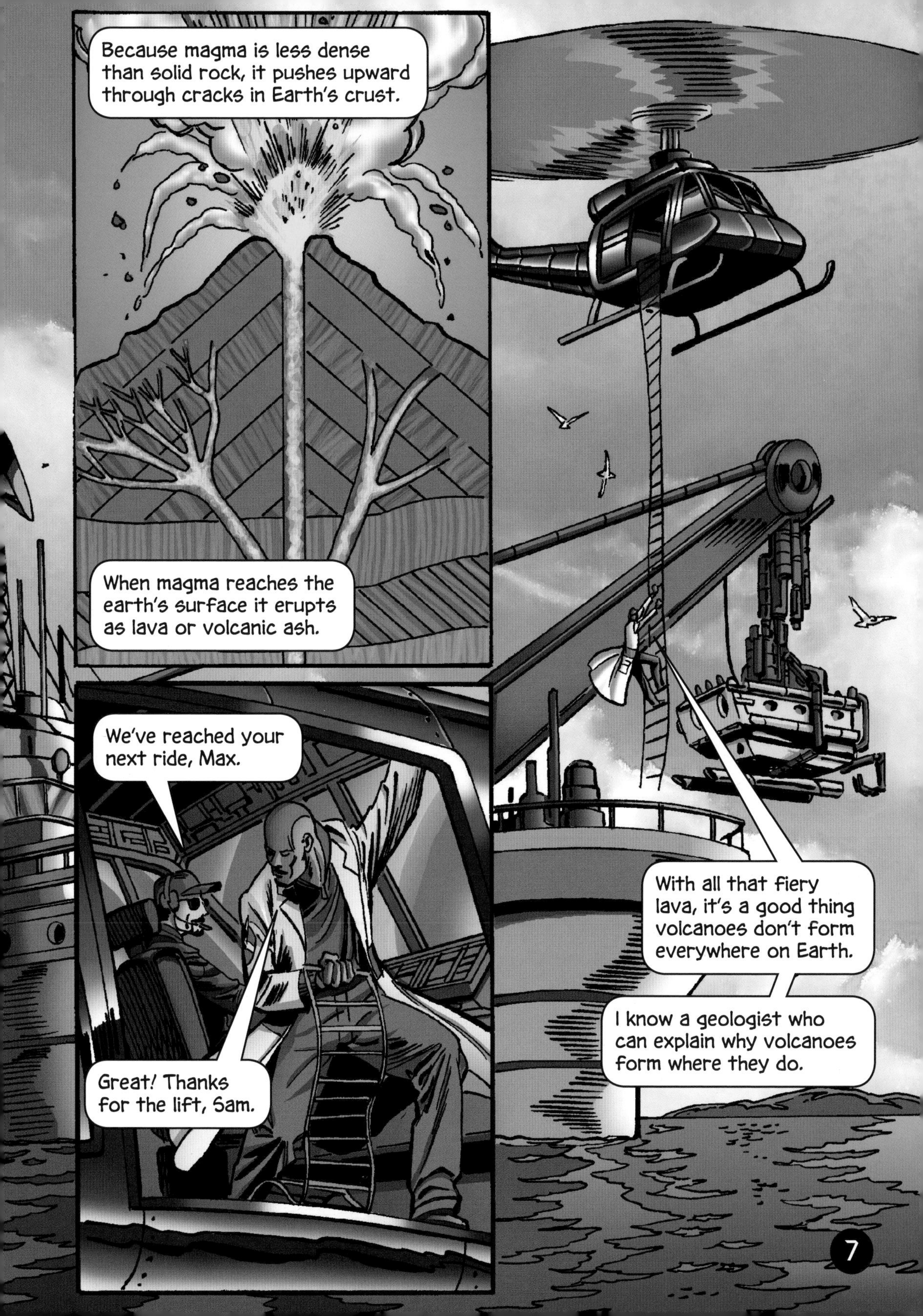
Because magma is less dense than solid rock, it pushes upward through cracks in Earth's crust.
When magma reaches the earth's surface it erupts as lava or volcanic ash.
We've reached your next ride, Max.
Great! Thanks for the lift, Sam.
With all that fiery lava, it's a good thing volcanoes don't form everywhere on Earth.
I know a geologist who can explain why volcanoes form where they do.

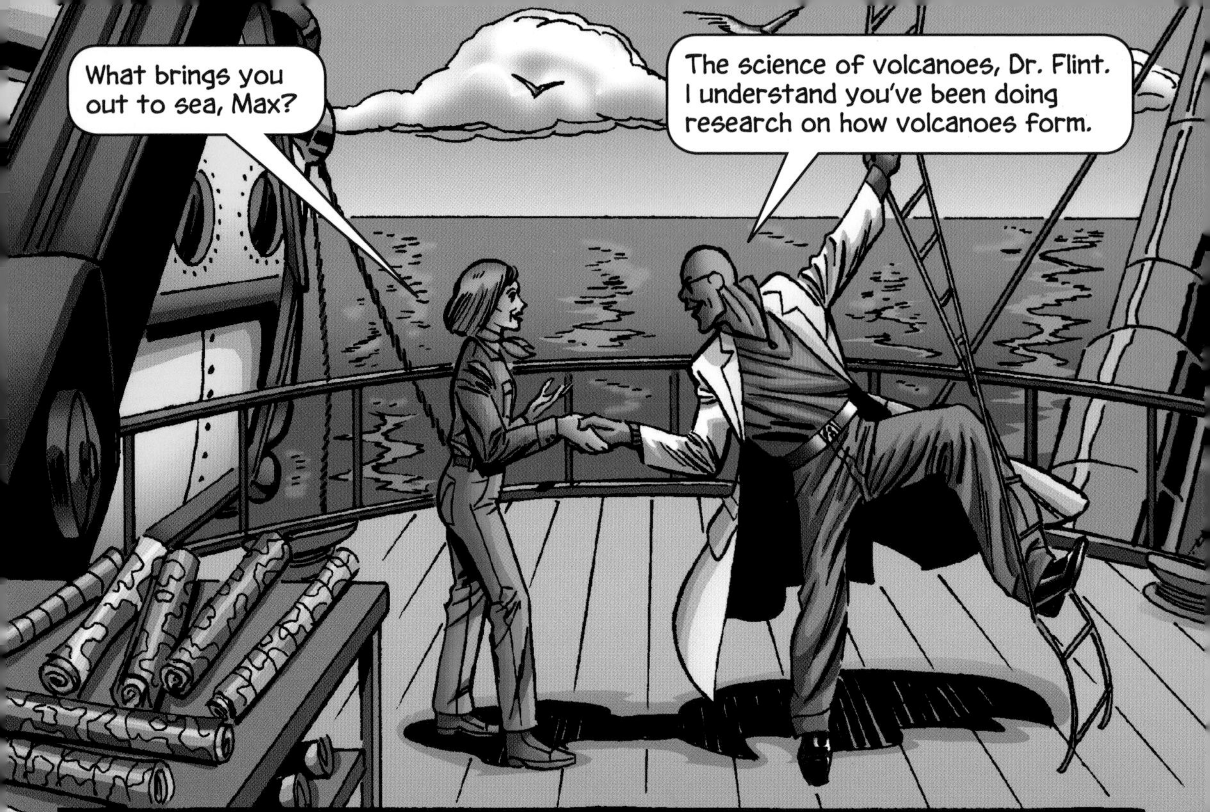
What brings you out to sea, Max?
The science of volcanoes, Dr. Flint. I understand you've been doing research on how volcanoes form.

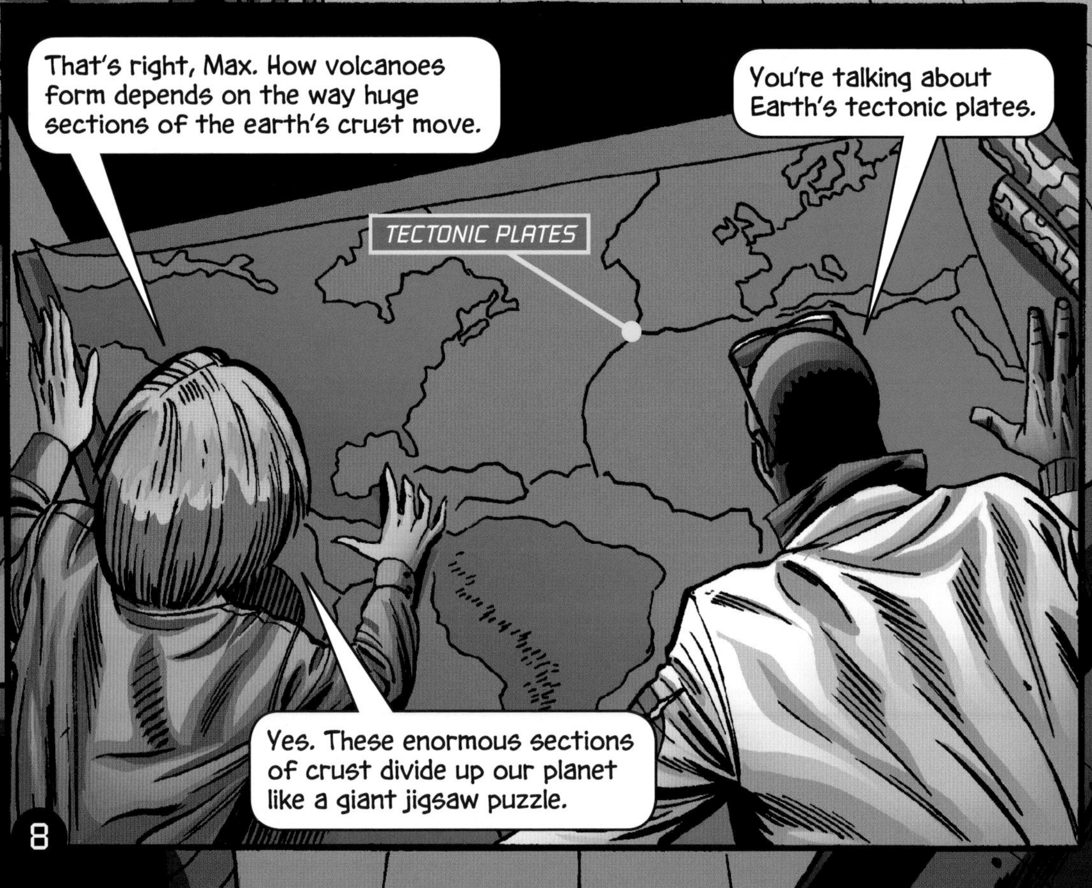
That's right, Max. How volcanoes form depends on the way huge sections of the earth's crust move.
You're talking about Earth's tectonic plates.
TECTONIC PLATES
Yes. These enormous sections of crust divide up our planet like a giant jigsaw puzzle.

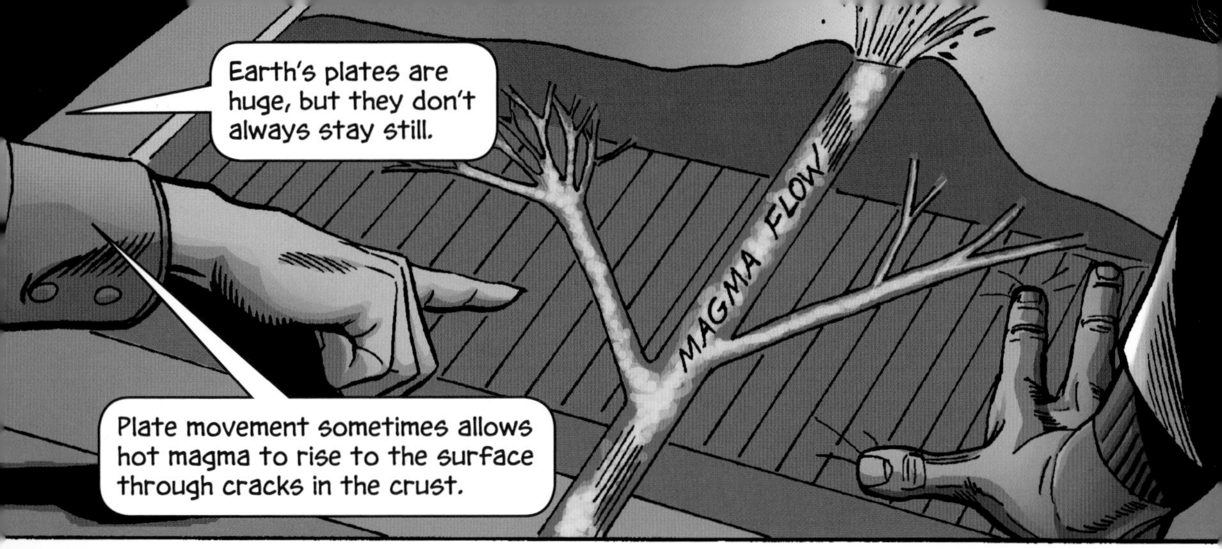
Earth's plates are huge, but they don't always stay still.
MAGMA FLOW
Plate movement sometimes allows hot magma to rise to the surface through cracks in the crust.

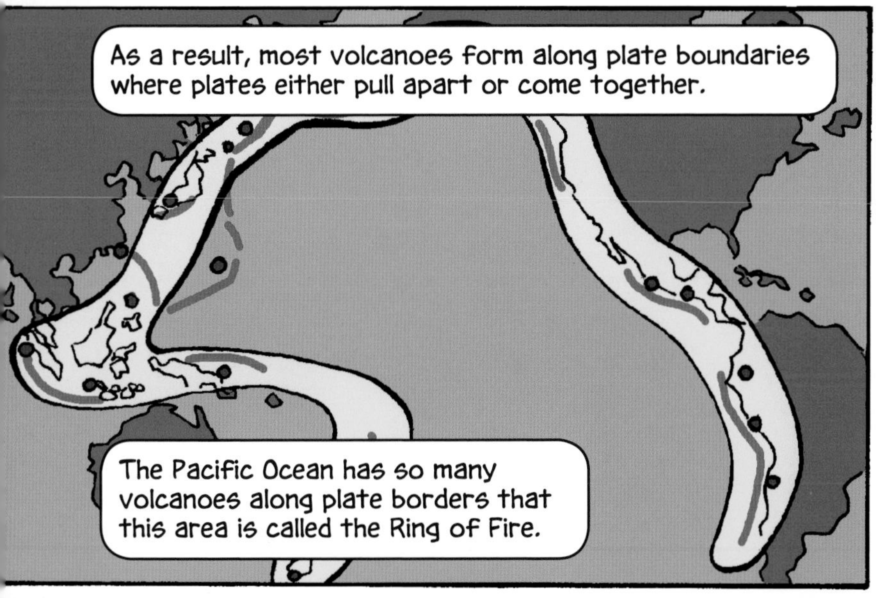
As a result, most volcanoes form along plate boundaries where plates either pull apart or come together.
The Pacific Ocean has so many volcanoes along plate borders that this area is called the Ring of Fire.

HOT SPOTS
Not all volcanoes form on plate boundaries. Some form when magma pushes its way through the middle of a tectonic plate. These areas are called hot spots. The Hawaiian Islands formed above a hot spot in the middle of the Pacific Plate.

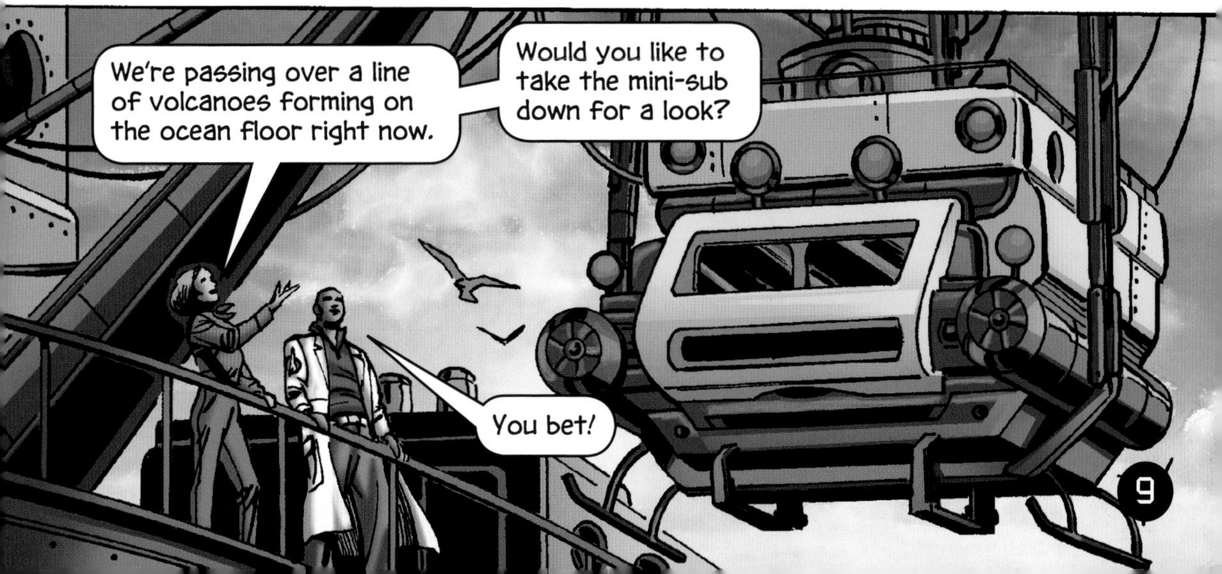
We're passing over a line of volcanoes forming on the ocean floor right now.
Would you like to take the mini-sub down for a look?
You bet!

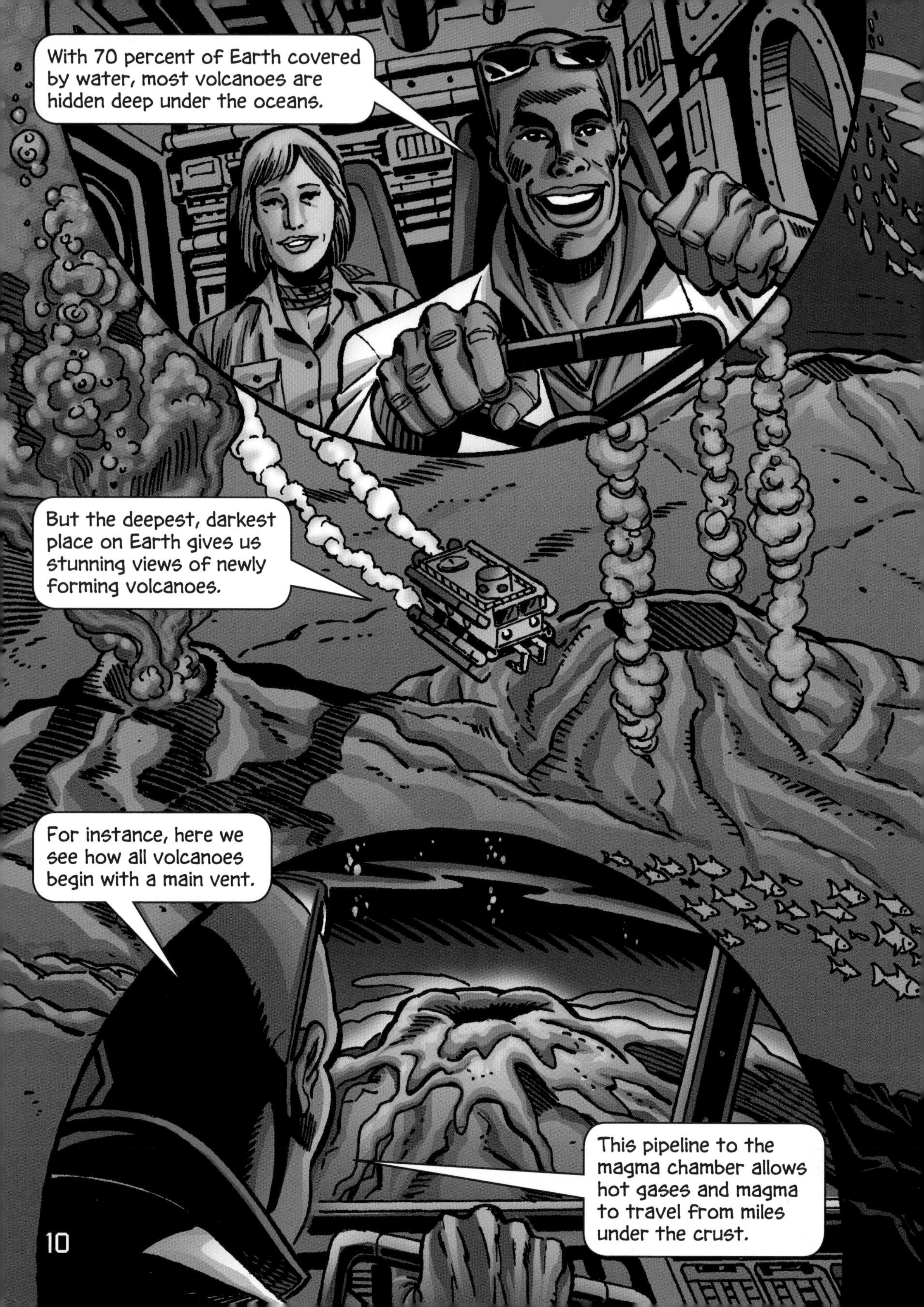

With 70 percent of Earth covered by water, most volcanoes are hidden deep under the oceans.
But the deepest, darkest place on Earth gives us stunning views of newly forming volcanoes.
For instance, here we see how all volcanoes begin with a main vent.
This pipeline to the magma chamber allows hot gases and magma to travel from miles under the crust.

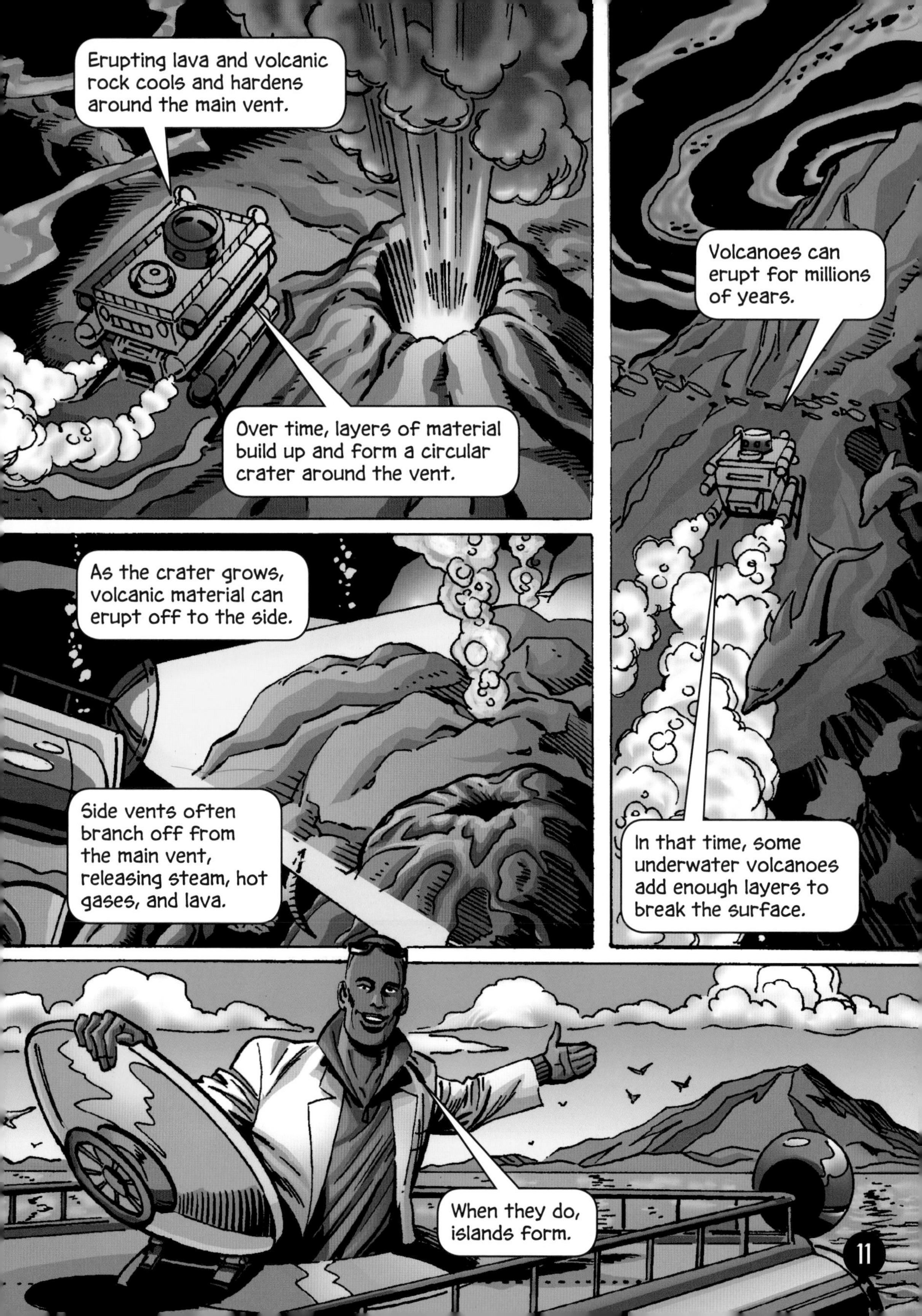
Erupting lava and volcanic rock cools and hardens around the main vent.
Over time, layers of material build up and form a circular crater around the vent.
Volcanoes can erupt for millions of years.
As the crater grows, volcanic material can erupt off to the side.
Side vents often branch off from the main vent, releasing steam, hot gases, and lava.
In that time, some underwater volcanoes add enough layers to break the surface.
When they do, islands form.

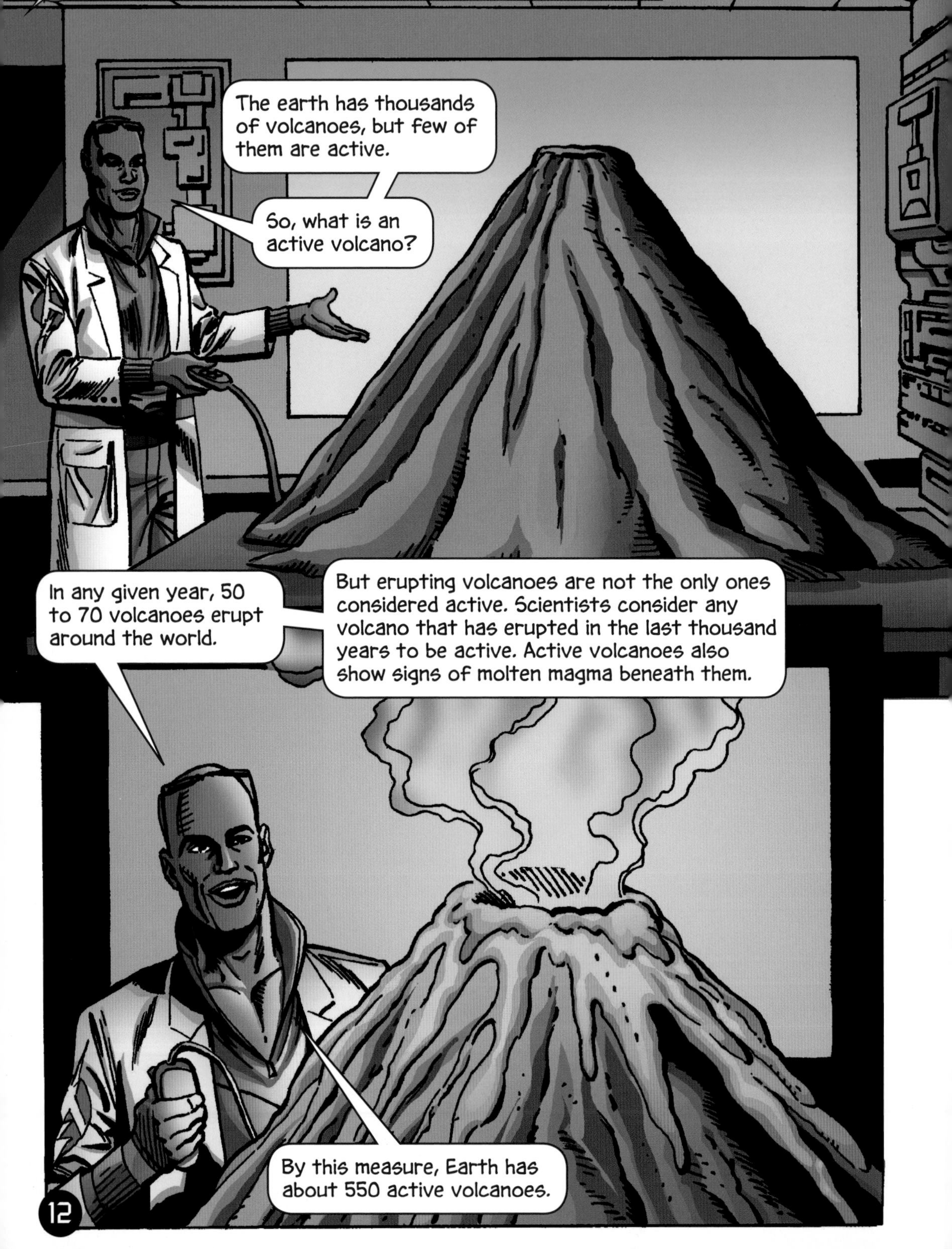
The earth has thousands of volcanoes, but few of them are active.
So, what is an active volcano?
In any given year, 50 to 70 volcanoes erupt around the world.
But erupting volcanoes are not the only ones considered active. Scientists consider any volcano that has erupted in the last thousand years to be active. Active volcanoes also show signs of molten magma beneath them.
By this measure, Earth has about 550 active volcanoes.

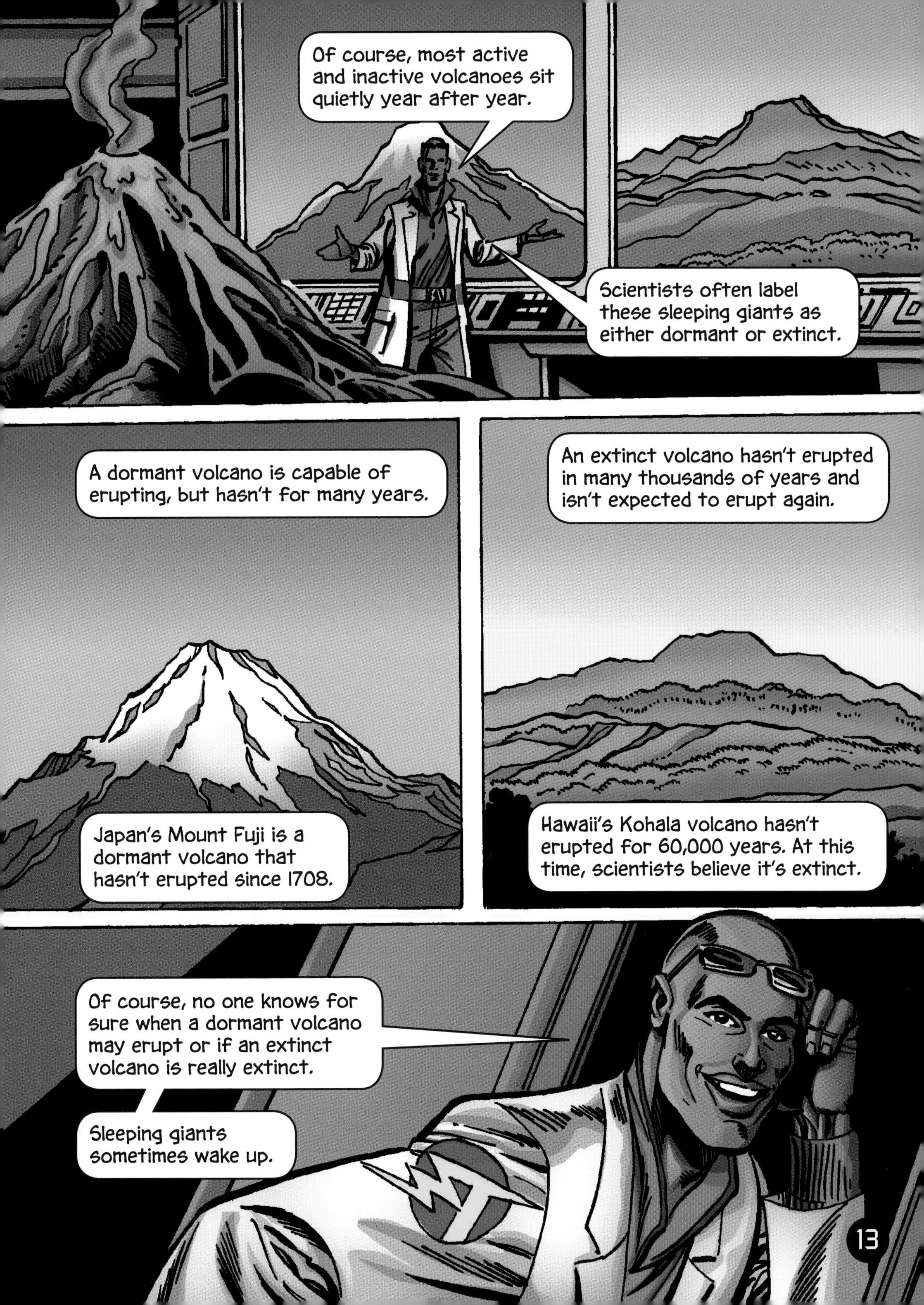
Of course, most active and inactive volcanoes sit quietly year after year.
Scientists often label these sleeping giants as either dormant or extinct.
A dormant volcano is capable of erupting, but hasn't for many years.
Japan's Mount Fuji is a dormant volcano that hasn't erupted since 1708.
An extinct volcano hasn't erupted in many thousands of years and isn't expected to erupt again.
Hawaii's Kohala volcano hasn't erupted for 60,000 years. At this time, scientists believe it's extinct.
Of course, no one knows for sure when a dormant volcano may erupt or if an extinct volcano is really extinct.
Sleeping giants sometimes wake up.

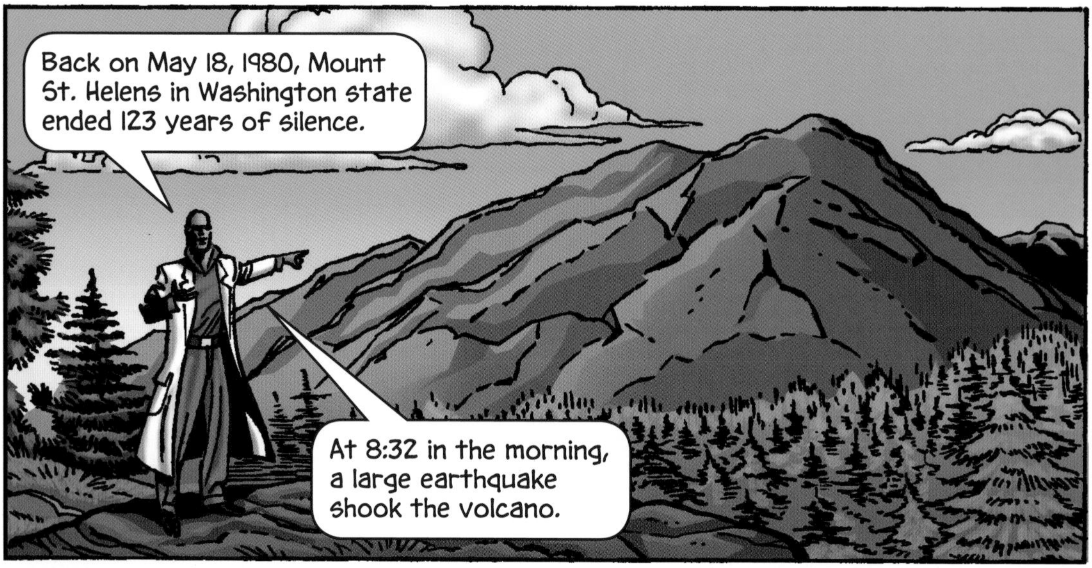
Back on May 18, 1980, Mount St. Helens in Washington state ended 123 years of silence.
At 8:32 in the morning, a large earthquake shook the volcano.

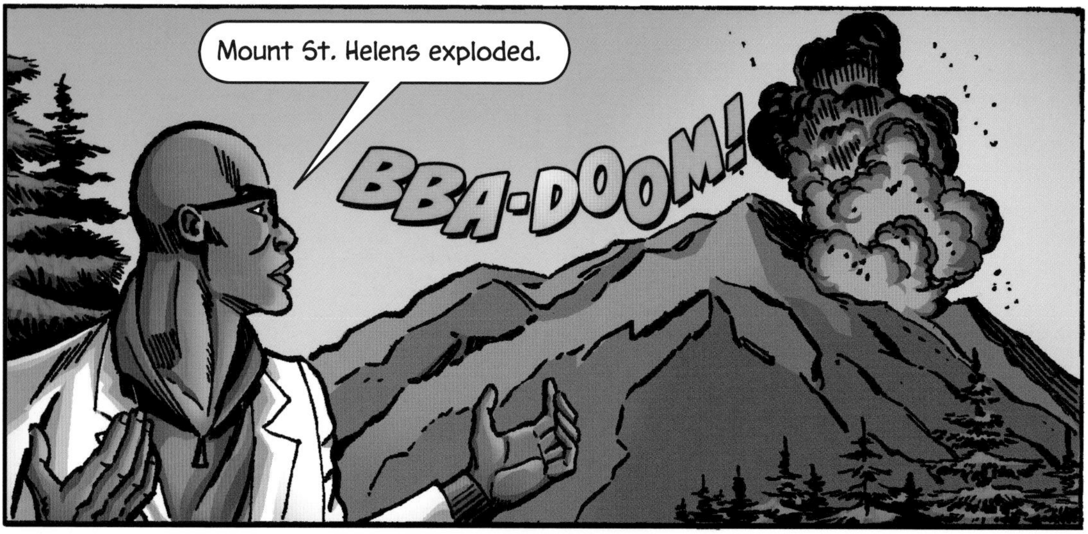
Mount St. Helens exploded.
BBA-DOOM!

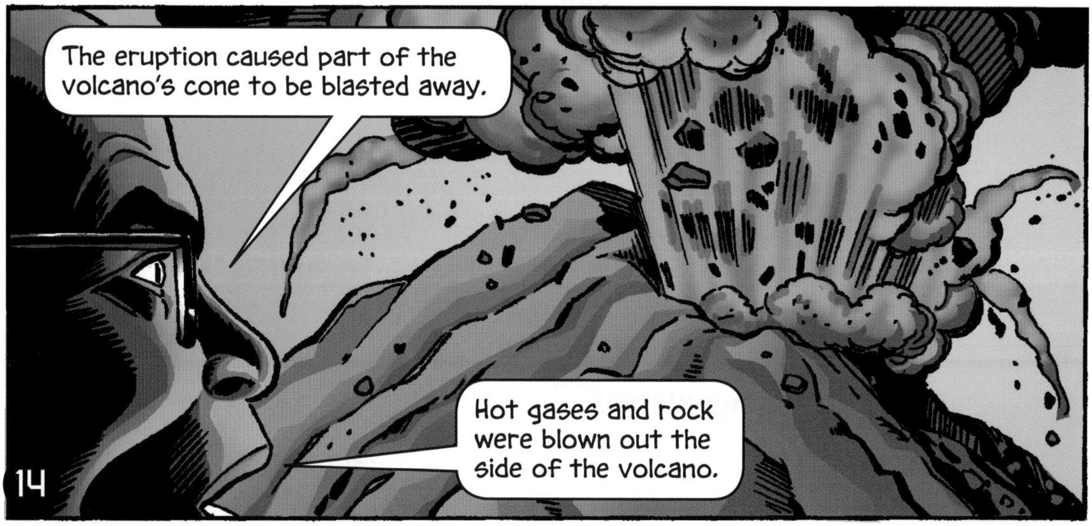
The eruption caused part of the volcano's cone to be blasted away.
Hot gases and rock were blown out the side of the volcano.

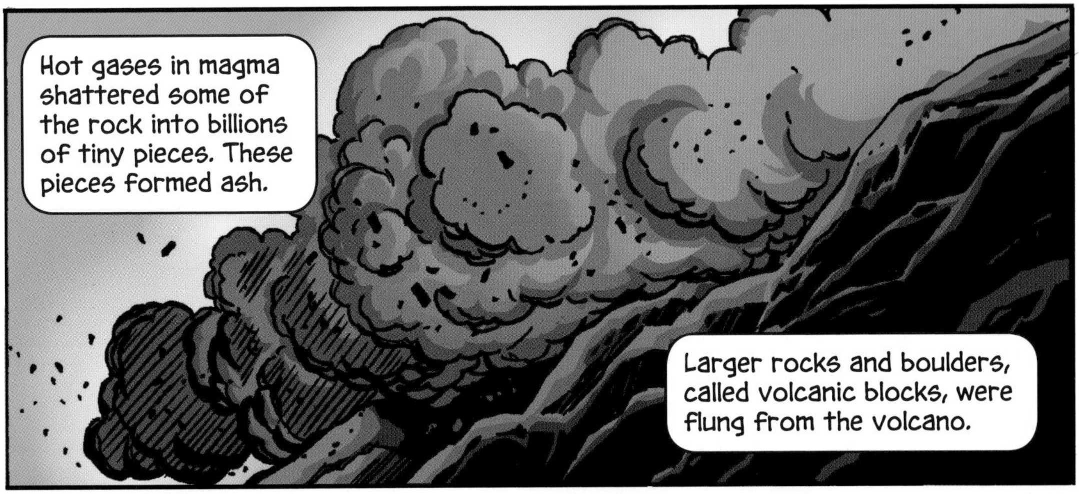
Hot gases in magma shattered some of the rock into billions of tiny pieces. These pieces formed ash.
Larger rocks and boulders, called volcanic blocks, were flung from the volcano.

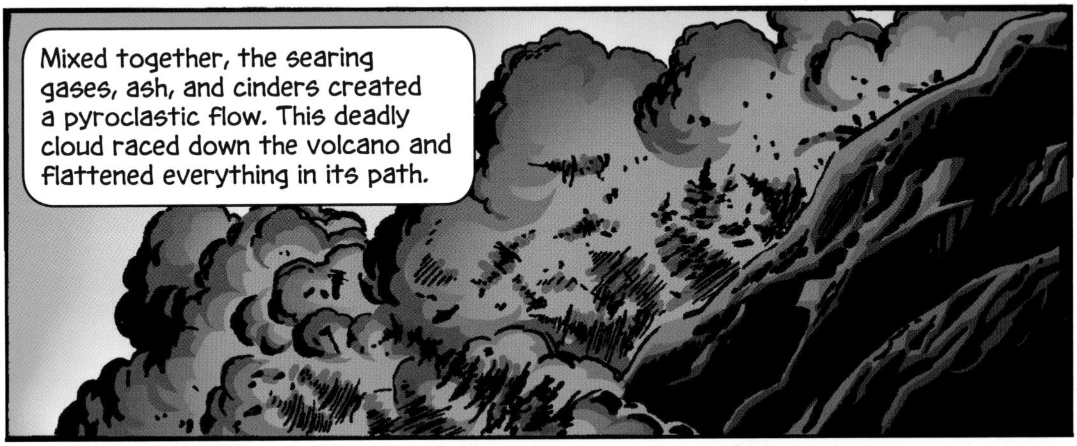
Mixed together, the searing gases, ash, and cinders created a pyroclastic flow. This deadly cloud raced down the volcano and flattened everything in its path.

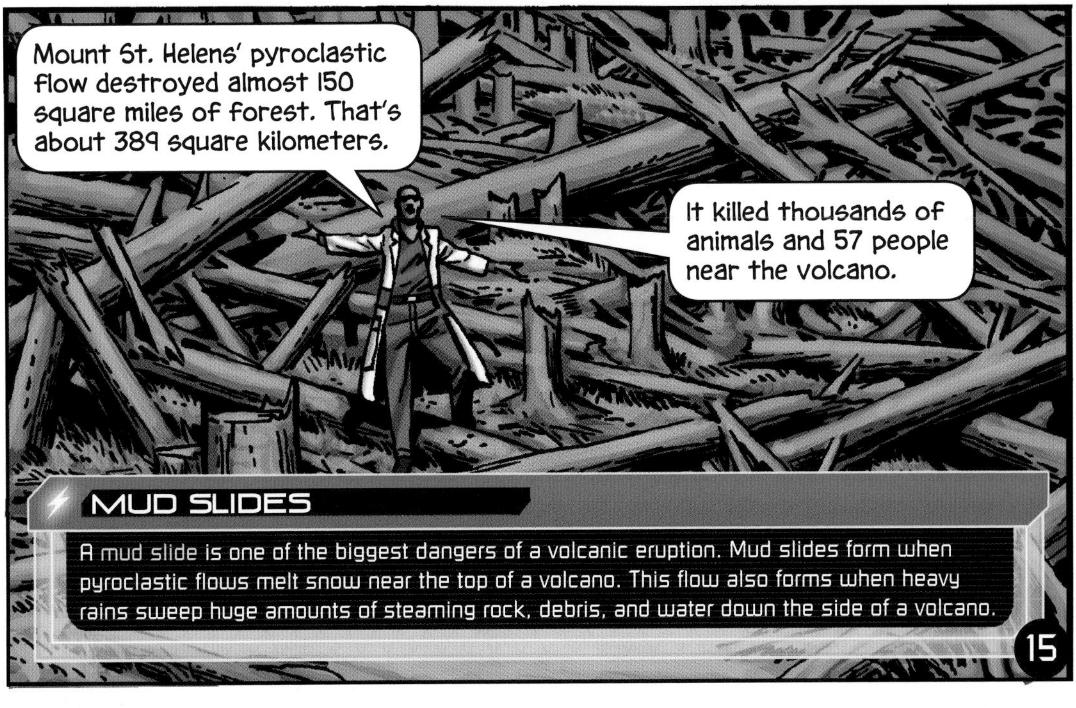
Mount St. Helens' pyroclastic flow destroyed almost 150 square miles of forest. That's about 389 square kilometers.
It killed thousands of animals and 57 people near the volcano.

MUD SLIDES

A mud slide is one of the biggest dangers of a volcanic eruption. Mud slides form when pyroclastic flows melt snow near the top of a volcano. This flow also forms when heavy rains sweep huge amounts of steaming rock, debris, and water down the side of a volcano.

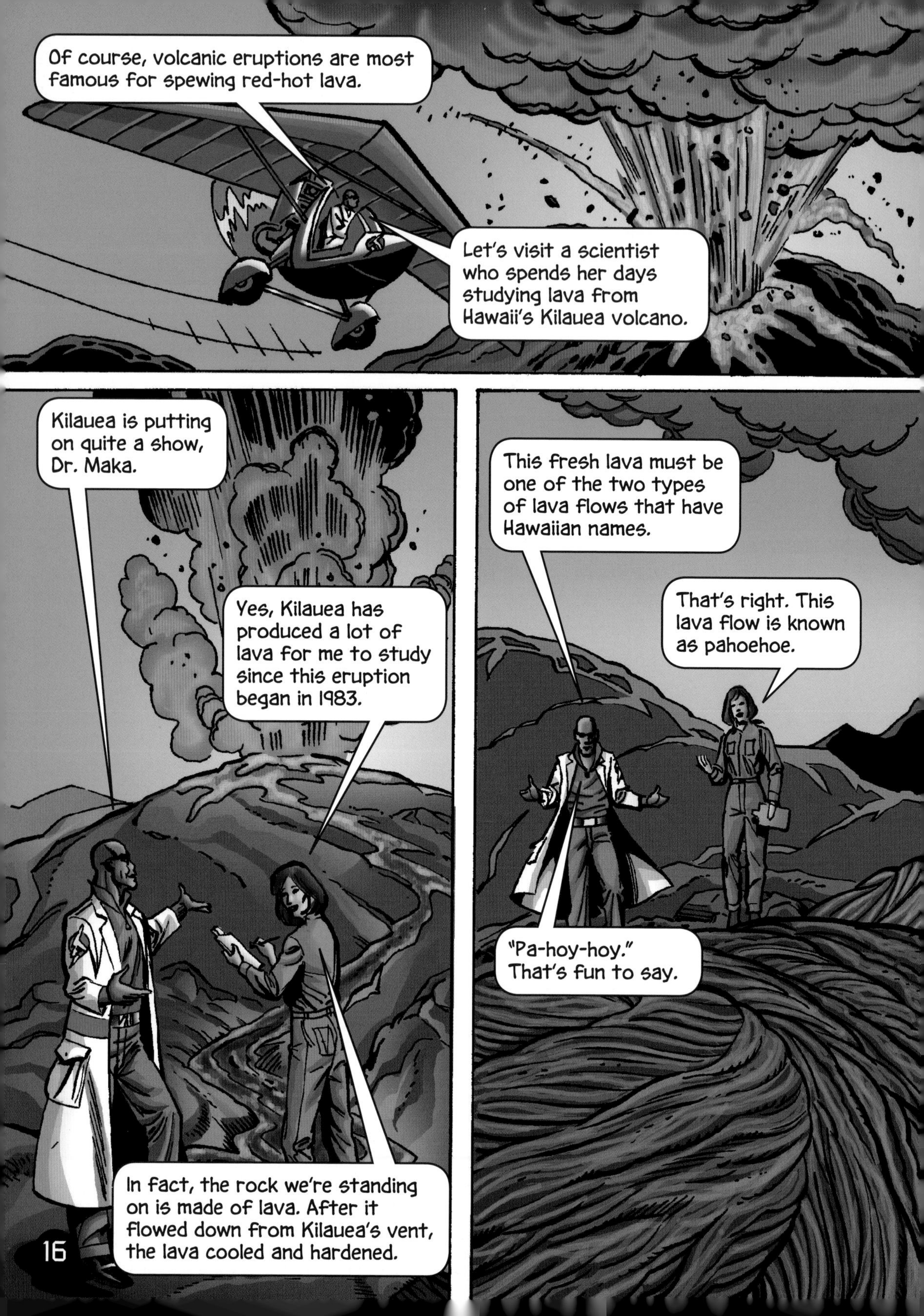
Of course, volcanic eruptions are most famous for spewing red-hot lava.
Let's visit a scientist who spends her days studying lava from Hawaii's Kilauea volcano.
Kilauea is putting on quite a show, Dr. Maka.
Yes, Kilauea has produced a lot of lava for me to study since this eruption began in 1983.
In fact, the rock we're standing on is made of lava. After it flowed down from Kilauea's vent, the lava cooled and hardened.
This fresh lava must be one of the two types of lava flows that have Hawaiian names.
That's right. This lava flow is known as pahoehoe.
"Pa-hoy-hoy." That's fun to say.

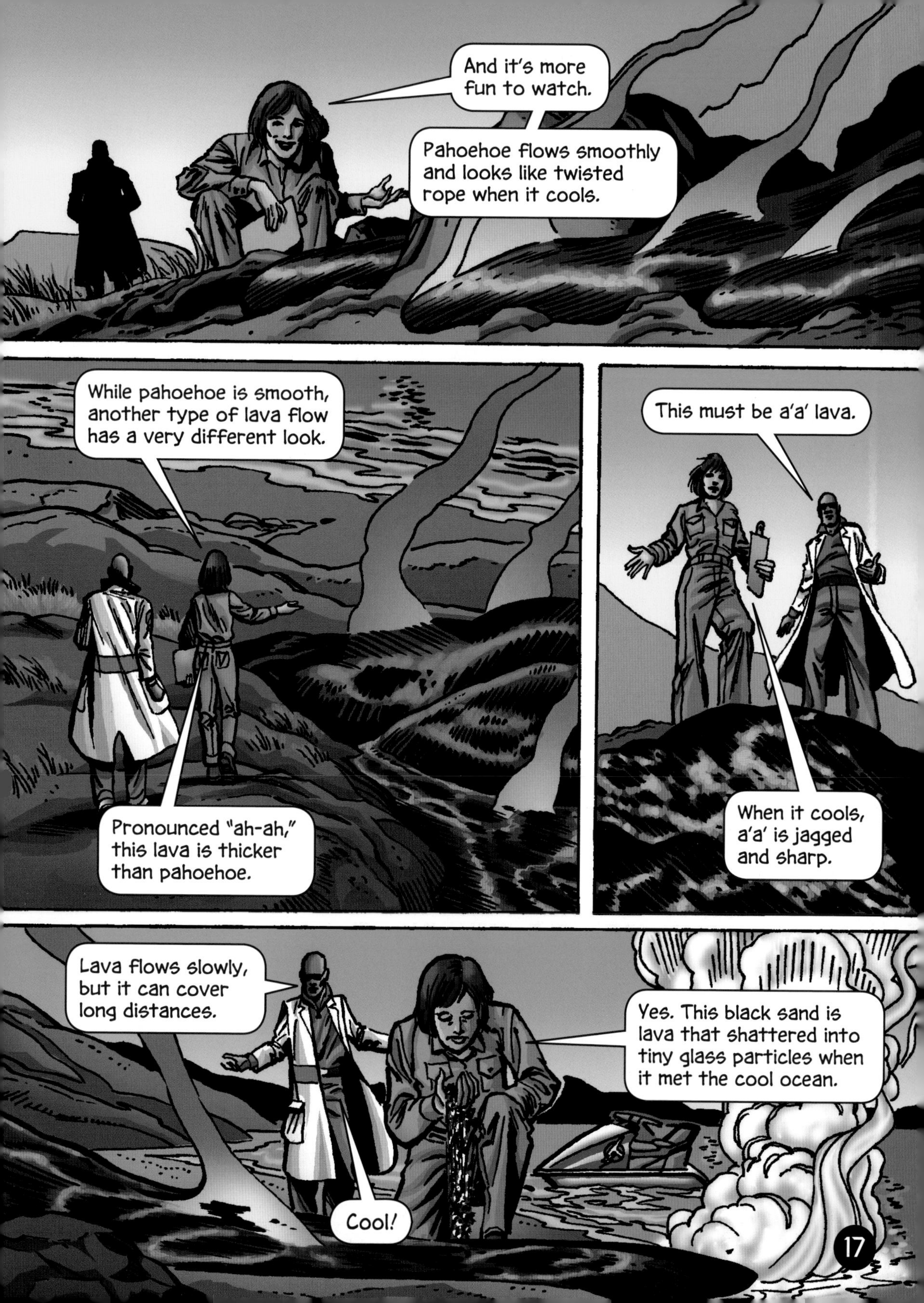

And it's more fun to watch.
Pahoehoe flows smoothly and looks like twisted rope when it cools.
While pahoehoe is smooth, another type of lava flow has a very different look.
Pronounced "ah-ah," this lava is thicker than pahoehoe.
This must be a'a' lava.
When it cools, a'a' is jagged and sharp.
Lava flows slowly, but it can cover long distances.
Yes. This black sand is lava that shattered into tiny glass particles when it met the cool ocean.
Cool!

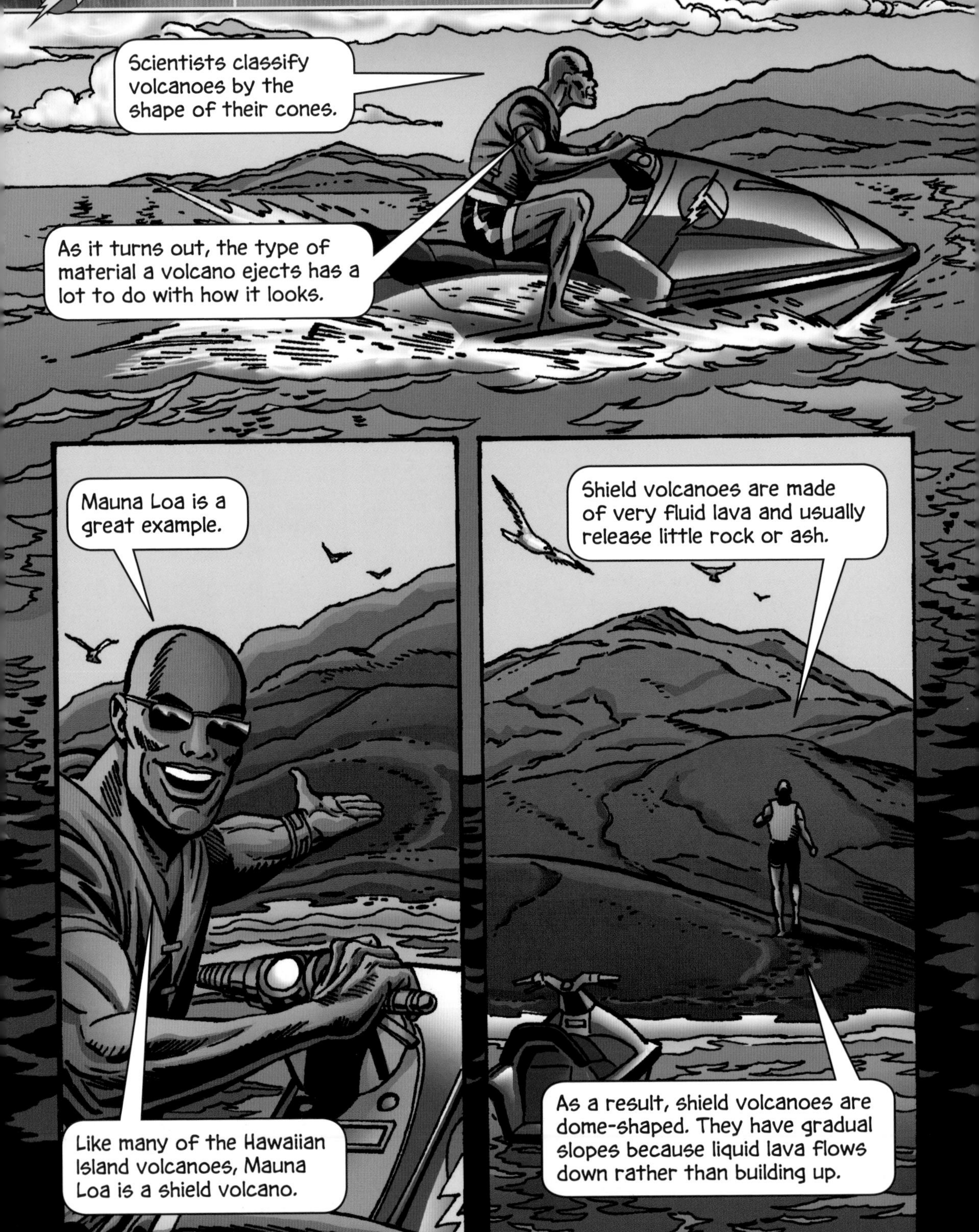
Scientists classify volcanoes by the shape of their cones.
As it turns out, the type of material a volcano ejects has a lot to do with how it looks.
Mauna Loa is a great example.
Like many of the Hawaiian Island volcanoes, Mauna Loa is a shield volcano.
Shield volcanoes are made of very fluid lava and usually release little rock or ash.
As a result, shield volcanoes are dome-shaped. They have gradual slopes because liquid lava flows down rather than building up.

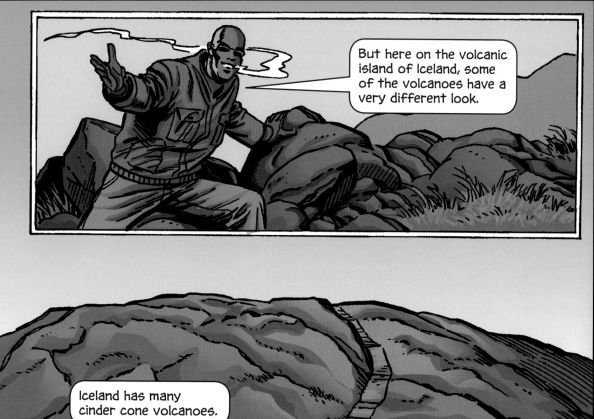

But here on the volcanic island of Iceland, some of the volcanoes have a very different look.

Iceland has many cinder cone volcanoes.

Cinder cones are usually smaller and much steeper than shield volcanoes. They form when globs of lava are thrown into the air by an eruption.

As the lava globs fall, they break apart and cool into cinders that pile up around the volcano's central vent.

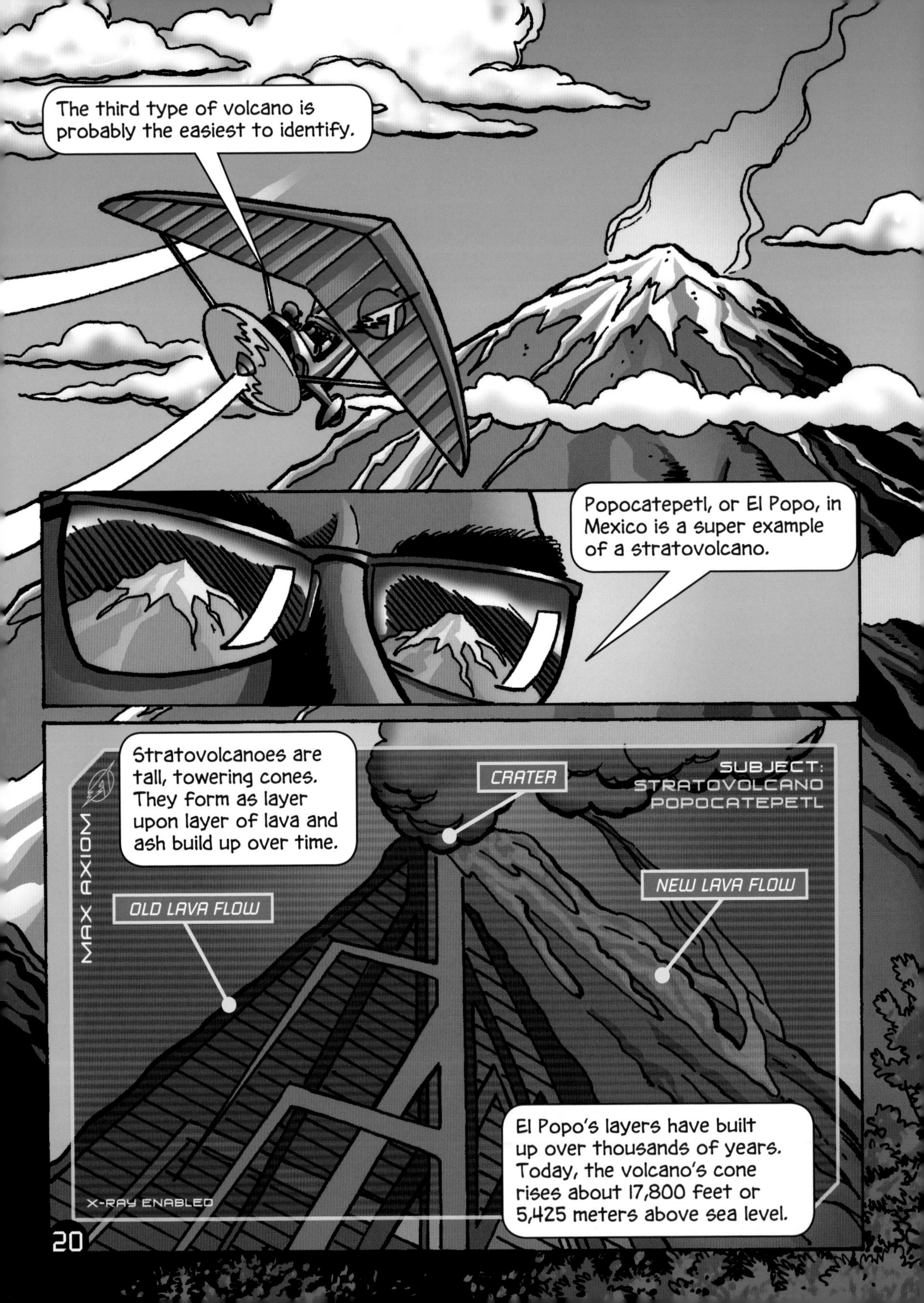

The third type of volcano is probably the easiest to identify.
Popocatepetl, or El Popo, in Mexico is a super example of a stratovolcano.
MAX AXIOM
Stratovolcanoes are tall, towering cones. They form as layer upon layer of lava and ash build up over time.
CRATER
SUBJECT: STRATOVOLCANO POPOCATEPETL
OLD LAVA FLOW
NEW LAVA FLOW
X-RAY ENABLED
El Popo's layers have built up over thousands of years. Today, the volcano's cone rises about 17,800 feet or 5,425 meters above sea level.

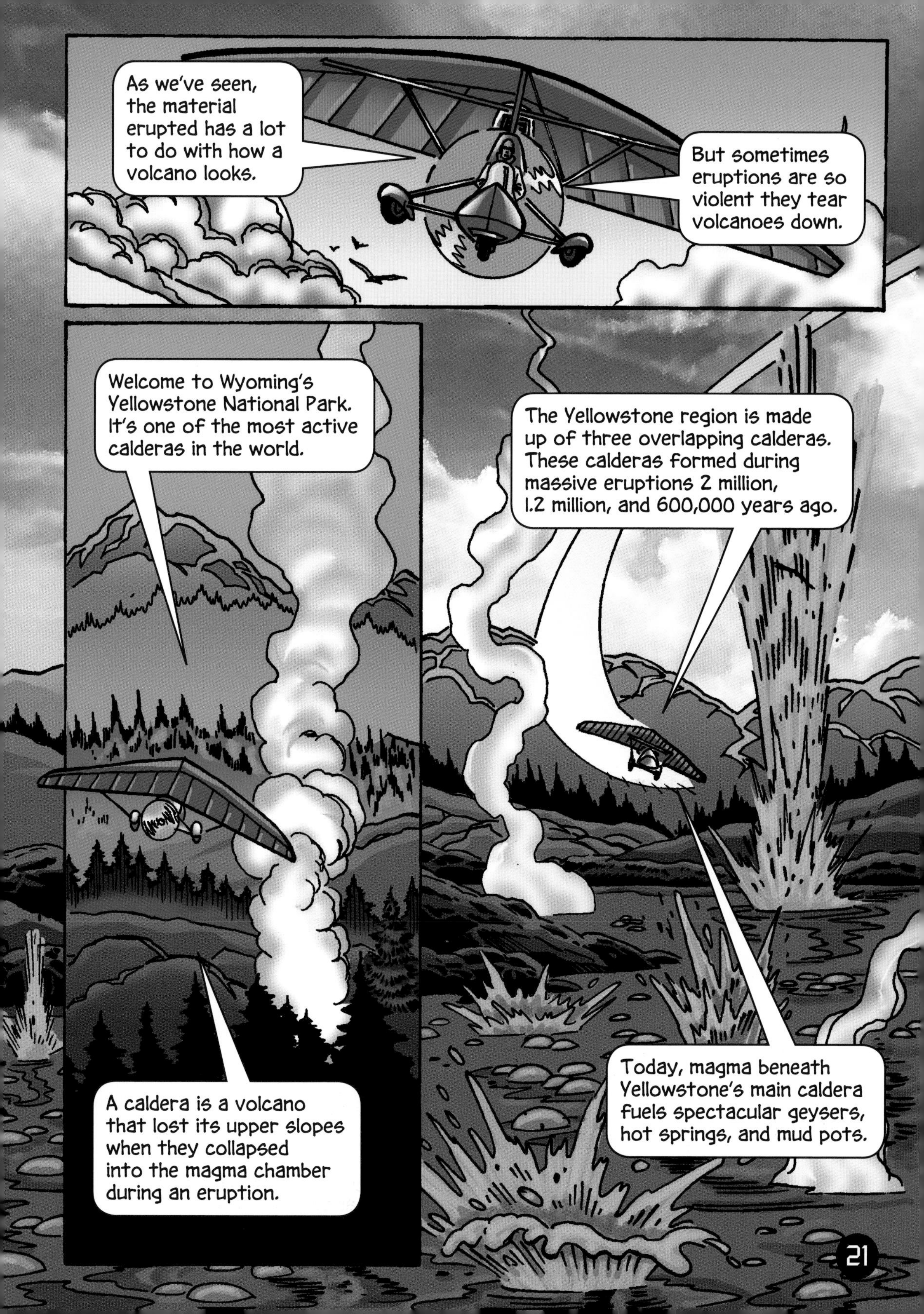
As we've seen, the material erupted has a lot to do with how a volcano looks.
But sometimes eruptions are so violent they tear volcanoes down.
Welcome to Wyoming's Yellowstone National Park. It's one of the most active calderas in the world.
A caldera is a volcano that lost its upper slopes when they collapsed into the magma chamber during an eruption.
The Yellowstone region is made up of three overlapping calderas. These calderas formed during massive eruptions 2 million, 1.2 million, and 600,000 years ago.
Today, magma beneath Yellowstone's main caldera fuels spectacular geysers, hot springs, and mud pots.

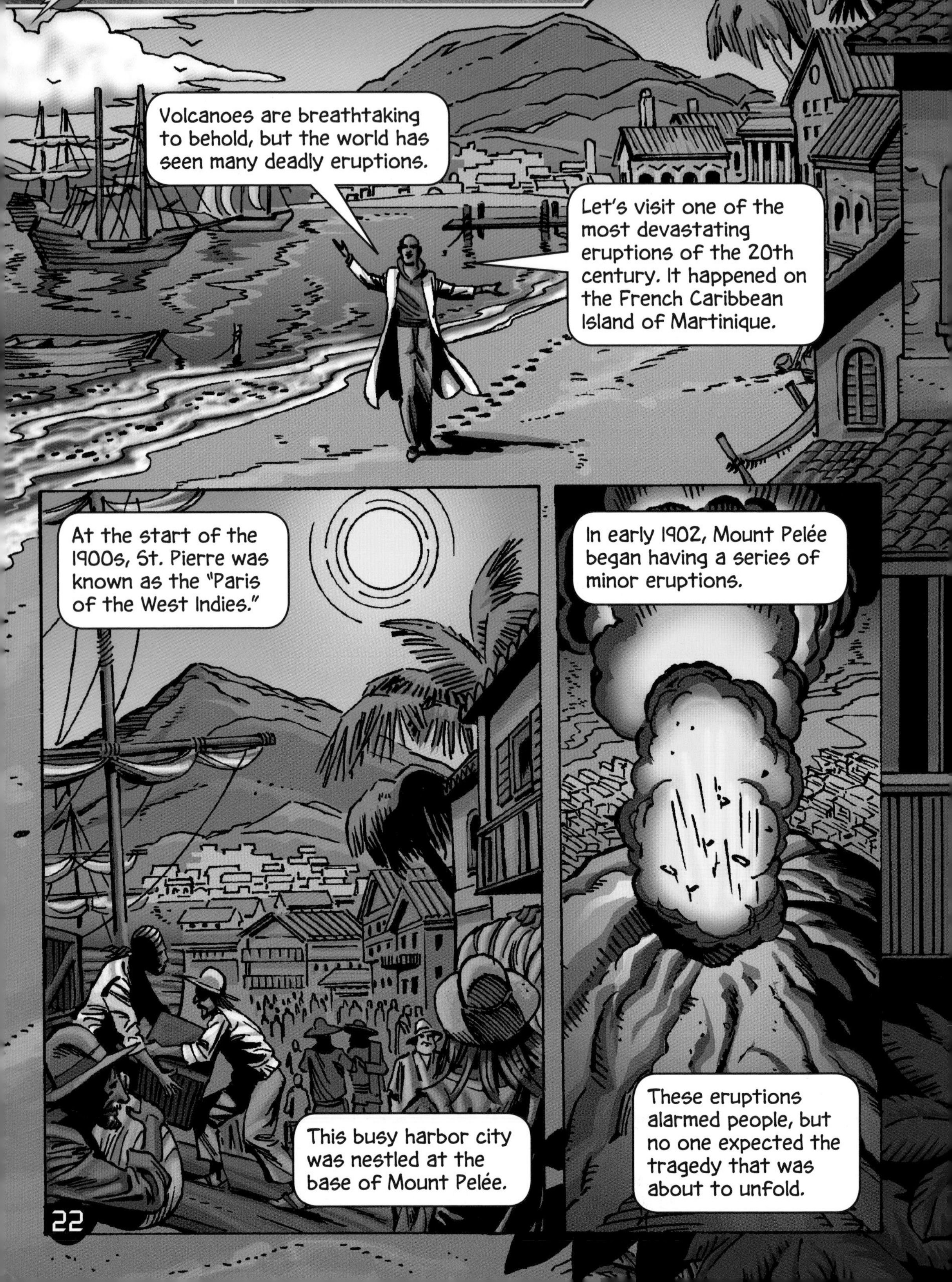
Volcanoes are breathtaking to behold, but the world has seen many deadly eruptions.
Let's visit one of the most devastating eruptions of the 20th century. It happened on the French Caribbean Island of Martinique.
At the start of the 1900s, St. Pierre was known as the "Paris of the West Indies."
This busy harbor city was nestled at the base of Mount Pelée.
In early 1902, Mount Pelée began having a series of minor eruptions.
These eruptions alarmed people, but no one expected the tragedy that was about to unfold.

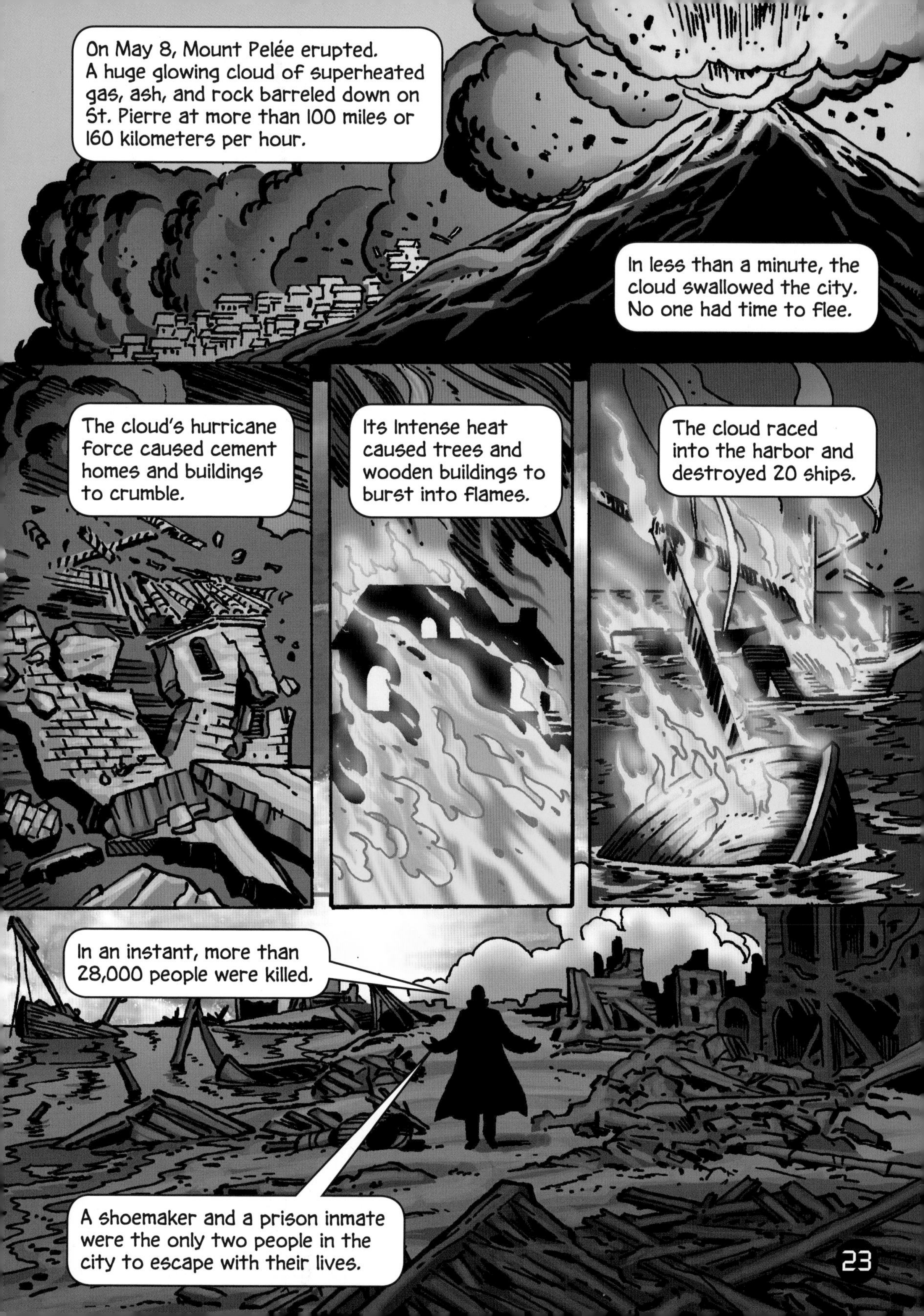
On May 8, Mount Pelée erupted. A huge glowing cloud of superheated gas, ash, and rock barreled down on St. Pierre at more than 100 miles or 160 kilometers per hour.
In less than a minute, the cloud swallowed the city. No one had time to flee.
The cloud's hurricane force caused cement homes and buildings to crumble.
Its intense heat caused trees and wooden buildings to burst into flames.
The cloud raced into the harbor and destroyed 20 ships.
In an instant, more than 28,000 people were killed.
A shoemaker and a prison inmate were the only two people in the city to escape with their lives.

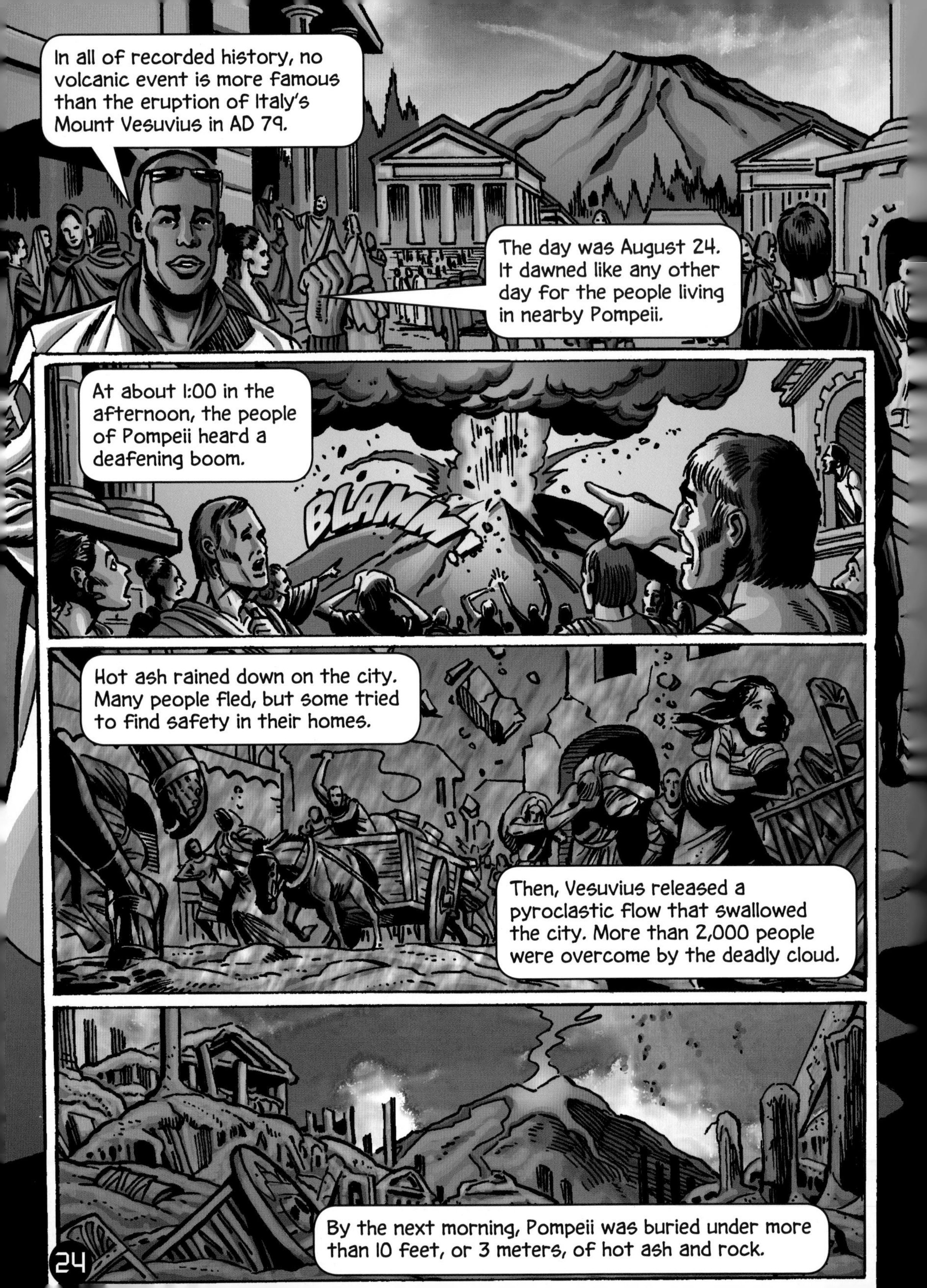
In all of recorded history, no volcanic event is more famous than the eruption of Italy's Mount Vesuvius in AD 79.
The day was August 24. It dawned like any other day for the people living in nearby Pompeii.
At about 1:00 in the afternoon, the people of Pompeii heard a deafening boom.
BLAMM
Hot ash rained down on the city. Many people fled, but some tried to find safety in their homes.
Then, Vesuvius released a pyroclastic flow that swallowed the city. More than 2,000 people were overcome by the deadly cloud.
By the next morning, Pompeii was buried under more than 10 feet, or 3 meters, of hot ash and rock.

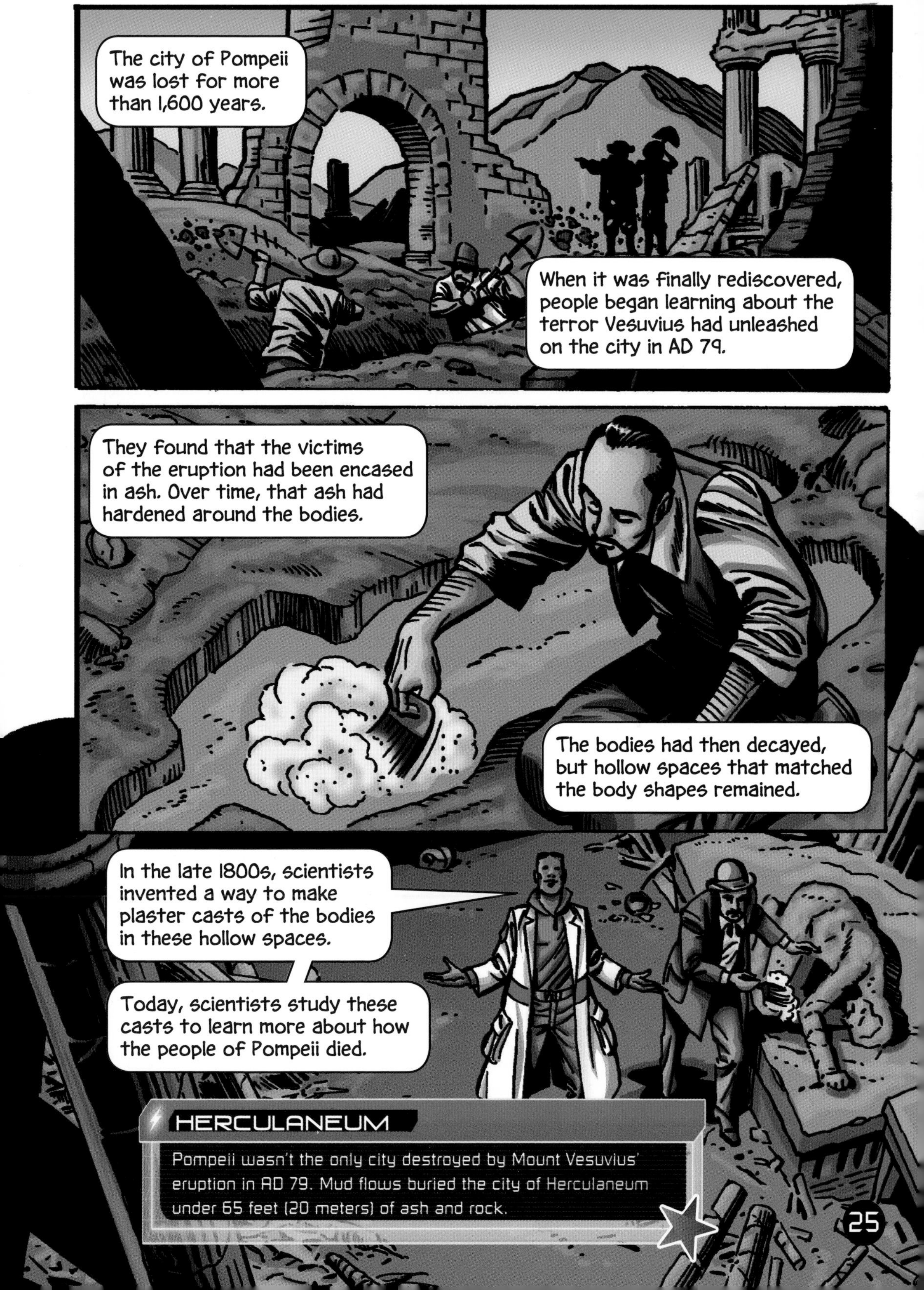
The city of Pompeii was lost for more than 1,600 years.
When it was finally rediscovered, people began learning about the terror Vesuvius had unleashed on the city in AD 79.
They found that the victims of the eruption had been encased in ash. Over time, that ash had hardened around the bodies.
The bodies had then decayed, but hollow spaces that matched the body shapes remained.
In the late 1800s, scientists invented a way to make plaster casts of the bodies in these hollow spaces.
Today, scientists study these casts to learn more about how the people of Pompeii died.
HERCULANEUM
Pompeii wasn't the only city destroyed by Mount Vesuvius' eruption in AD 79. Mud flows buried the city of Herculaneum under 65 feet (20 meters) of ash and rock.

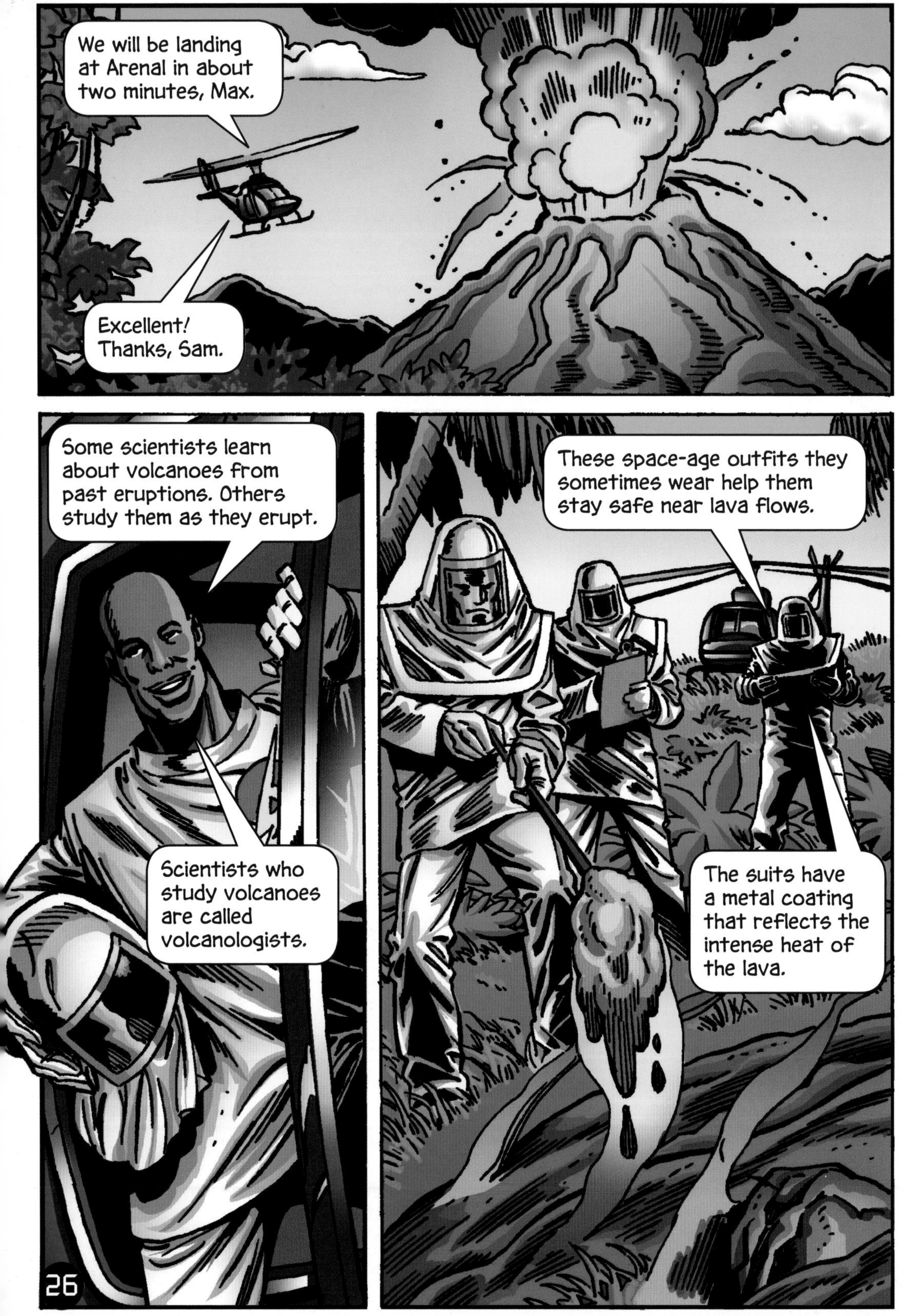

We will be landing at Arenal in about two minutes, Max.
Excellent! Thanks, Sam.
Some scientists learn about volcanoes from past eruptions. Others study them as they erupt.
Scientists who study volcanoes are called volcanologists.
These space-age outfits they sometimes wear help them stay safe near lava flows.
The suits have a metal coating that reflects the intense heat of the lava.

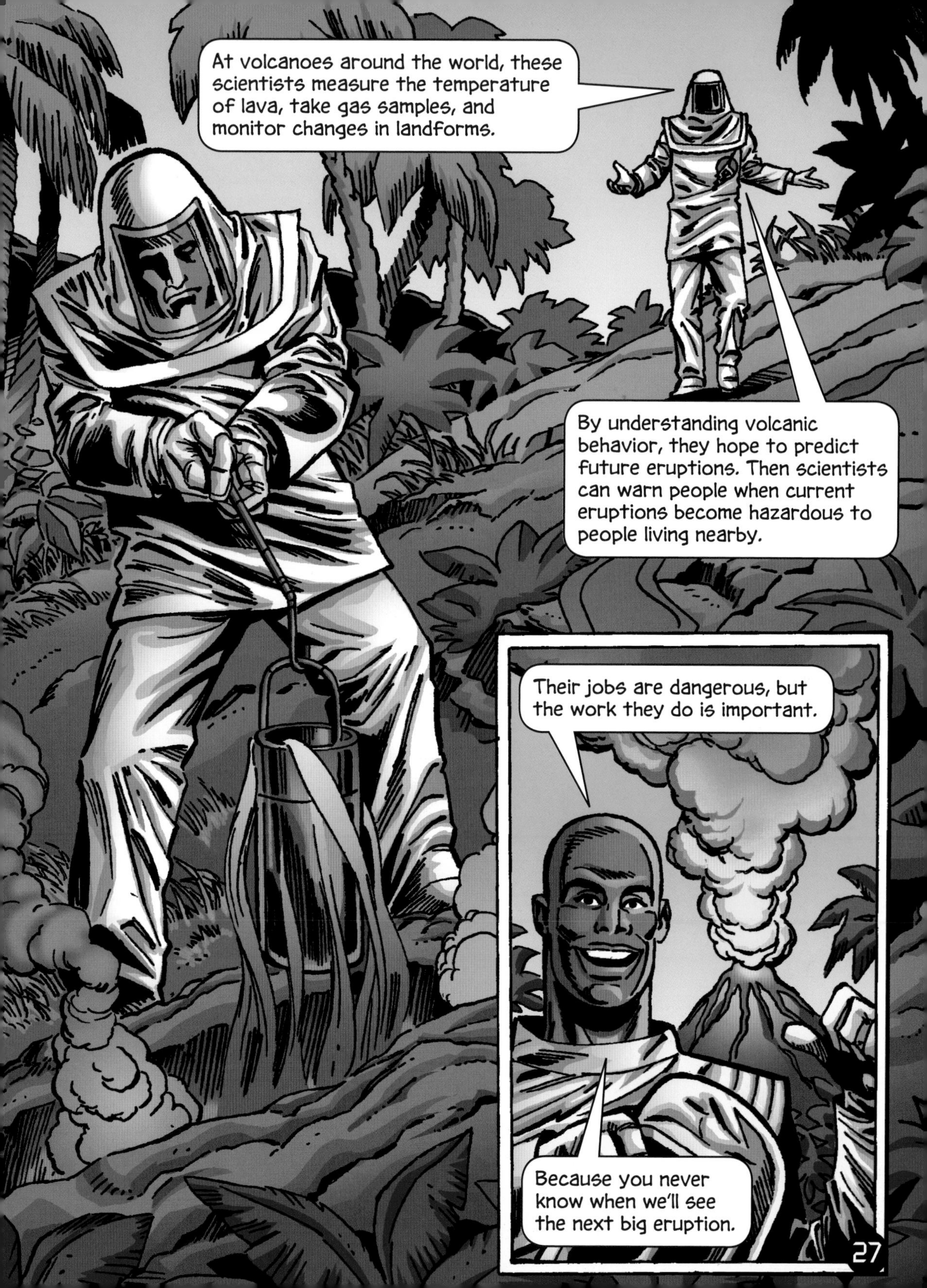
At volcanoes around the world, these scientists measure the temperature of lava, take gas samples, and monitor changes in landforms.
By understanding volcanic behavior, they hope to predict future eruptions. Then scientists can warn people when current eruptions become hazardous to people living nearby.
Their jobs are dangerous, but the work they do is important.
Because you never know when we'll see the next big eruption.

VOLCANOES

Lava and pyroclastic flows often destroy everything in their paths. Ash and lava carry many nutrients plants need to grow. After many years, hard lava flows become the soil plants and trees thrive on.

Lava is super hot, but it's not the most dangerous thing a volcano erupts. Lava usually moves so slowly that people have time to get out of its way. Huge mud slides and heated clouds of ash and gases are much more dangerous for people living near an eruption.

In October 2004, Mount St. Helens began erupting again. Although the eruptions were minor, the new activity pushed a massive rock slab out of the crater's dome. For a time, the rock slab stood about the length of a football field out of the crater.

In 1991, the eruption of Mount Pinatubo in the Philippines affected the weather around the world. Ash carried worldwide in the air blocked out some sunlight. In the year after the eruption, temperatures around the globe fell an average of 1 degree.

Iceland is one of the few places people can see two of Earth's plates spreading apart above sea level. Each year, the plates move apart about 1 inch (2.5 centimeters). As a result, Iceland has many active volcanoes, geysers, and hot springs.

Some scientists use space satellites to study volcanoes. Satellites measure heat released by a volcano and track eruption clouds as they travel around the globe.

Earth isn't the only place in our solar system where volcanoes have formed. Venus, Mars, and Jupiter's moon, Io, also have many volcanoes. In fact, Olympus Mons on Mars is the largest known volcano in the solar system. This huge shield volcano is about the size of the state of Arizona. It rises 15 miles (24 kilometers) above the surface of Mars.

Scientists use an electric thermometer to measure the temperature of lava. This thermometer is made of ceramic and stainless steel. These materials can stand up to lava's high temperatures.

SWEET LAVA FLOW

Let your mind flow as you experiment with the awe-inspiring properties of lava. Unlike real volcanic eruptions, this fun project ends with a sweet treat to eat!

WHAT YOU NEED:

- chocolate bar
- microwavable bowl
- spoon
- mini chocolate chips
- rainbow sprinkles
- paper
- pencil
- baking sheet

WHAT YOU DO:

1. Unwrap the chocolate bar and observe its properties. Is it hard or soft? Smooth or grainy?

2. Write your observations on your paper.

3. Drop the chocolate in the bowl.

4. Microwave on high for 30 seconds. Remove the bowl and take notes about what has happened to the chocolate.

5. Continue to microwave, 10 seconds at a time, until the chocolate is completely melted. Be careful not to boil or burn it.

6. Stir the melted chocolate. Add in a handful of mini chocolate chips and a handful of rainbow sprinkles.

7. Quickly and carefully spoon several globs of the mixture onto the baking sheet. Make sure to leave some room between the globs on the sheet.

8. Tilt the baking sheet slightly to let your lava "flow." Notice how tilting the pan creates the kind of slope you might find on the side of a volcano.

9. Watch the globs cool and note any changes on your paper. What do you think the chocolate chips and sprinkles represent? Also describe how this activity is similar to the way solid rock and lava responds to heating and cooling.

10. Eat your cooled lava flows while sharing your observations with a friend. Yum!

DISCUSSION QUESTIONS

1. Lava can be more than 2,000°F (1,000°C). Why are Max and Dr. Maka able to stand so close to the erupting volcano on page 16?

2. Volcanoes come in many shapes and sizes. Choose two kinds of volcanoes. What are the reasons for their differences?

3. A shield volcano has gentle slopes. What does this mean about its lava?

4. Mount Pelée caused a lot of destruction. What are at least three reasons why?

WRITING PROMPTS

1. A stratovolcano has many layers of lava. Create a diagram showing each layer and list what each is made of.

2. Max visits several volcanoes. Pick two and write a short paragraph comparing and contrasting their features and how they erupt.

3. Make a volcano chart with three columns labeled active, inactive, and dormant. List the main features and characteristics of each type of volcano in its column.

4. Write a news story about a volcano eruption featured in the book. Focus on making your news story exciting and informative for someone who didn't witness it in person.

TAKE A QUIZ!

GLOSSARY

caldera (kal-DER-ah)—a collapsed volcano

cinder (SIN-dur)—a cooled piece of lava from an erupting volcano

cone (KOHN)—the tip of a volcano

crust (KRUHST)—the thin outer layer of Earth's surface

dormant (DOR-muhnt)—not active; dormant volcanoes have not erupted for many years.

erupt (e-RUHPT)—to suddenly burst; a volcano shoots steam, lava, and ash into the air when it erupts

extinct (ek-STINGKT)—no longer active; a volcano is extinct if it has stopped erupting for thousands of years

lava (LAH-vuh)—the hot, liquid rock that pours out of a volcano when it erupts

magma (MAG-muh)—melted rock found beneath the surface of Earth

mantle (MAN-tuhl)—the layer of super-hot rock that surrounds Earth's core

molten (MOHLT-uhn)—melted by heat; lava is molten rock.

plate (PLAYT)—a large sheet of rock that is a piece of Earth's crust

pyroclastic flow (peye-roh-KLAS-tik FLOH)—a moving mixture of hot gases, ash, and rock from a volcano; a pyroclastic flow can reach speeds of up to 100 miles (161 km) per hour

vent (VENT)—a hole in a volcano; hot ash, steam, and lava blow out of vents from an erupting volcano

READ MORE

Howell, Izzi. *Volcano Geo Facts*. Geo Facts. New York: Crabtree Publishing Company, 2018.

Martin, Claudia. *Volcanoes and Earthquakes*. Discover Our World. Minneapolis, Minn.: Quarto Publishing Group USA, 2018.

Nargi, Lela. *Absolute Expert*: Volcanoes. Washington, D.C.: National Geographic Society, 2018.

INTERNET SITES

Use Facthound to find Internet sites related to this book.

Visit *www.facthound.com*

Just type in 9781543529470 and go!

 Check out projects, games and lots more at
www.capstonekids.com

INDEX